THE LITTLE RED BOOK

 Hazelden
Publishing

Hazelden Publishing
Center City, Minnesota 55012-0176
hazelden.org/bookstore

ISBN: 978-0-89486-985-3

Editor's note
The Twelve Steps and quotations from *Alcoholics Anonymous*
are reprinted with permission of Alcoholics Anonymous
World Services, Inc. Permission to reprint the Twelve Steps
does not mean that Alcoholics Anonymous has reviewed or
approved the contents of this publication, nor that AA agrees
with the views expressed herein. The views expressed herein
are solely those of the author. AA is a program of recovery
from alcoholism. Use of the Twelve Steps in connection with
programs and activities that are patterned after AA, but that
address other problems, does not imply otherwise.

Contents

Author's Note

The Little Red Book evolved from a series of notes originally prepared as Twelve Step suggestions for AA beginners. It aids in the study of the book *Alcoholics Anonymous* and contains many helpful topics for discussion meetings. Its distribution is prompted by a desire to "carry [the] message to alcoholics" in gratitude of our daily reprieve from insanity or alcoholic death.

Many groups, in meeting the AA need for instruction of new members, have adopted this brief summarization of the AA recovery program expounded in the Big Book, *Alcoholics Anonymous,** as an outline for study of that book. Worthwhile results have followed the inauguration of weekly classes devoted to guidance of new members in their quest for a better understanding of the Twelve Steps as a way of life for recovery from alcoholism.

These classes, directed by qualified members, have created a solidarity of understanding within our fellowship. They have brought a closer adherence to the Big Book, better understanding and application of

---

*The Big Book is *Alcoholics Anonymous,* 3d ed., published by A.A. World Services, Inc., New York, NY. Available through Hazelden Educational Materials, Center City, MN.

its philosophy, more effective sponsorship, and much higher ratio of sobriety among our members.

We hope *The Little Red Book* opens new avenues of thought and helps the AA member arrive at his or her successful interpretation of the program.

The Little Red Book makes frequent reference to basic matter in *Alcoholics Anonymous*, Third Edition.

DEDICATION

We sincerely dedicate this interpretation to

Bill W. and Dr. Bob

in appreciation of their tireless efforts and inspiration in making possible a *way of life* for alcoholics everywhere to recover from alcoholism. The hundreds of thousands who have recovered from this illness and those who are yet to be helped will ever be indebted to the founders of Alcoholics Anonymous for the unselfish service they have rendered to all alcoholics.

We believe our founders were inspired by a *Power greater than themselves* as they pioneered the Alcoholics Anonymous fellowship, wrote and edited *Alcoholics Anonymous,* and exemplified in their daily living the philosophy of its recovery program.

INTRODUCTION

This introduction to the Twelve Steps of the Alcoholics Anonymous program is offered to all alcoholic men and women whose "lives have become unmanageable" because of their powerlessness over alcohol.

The purpose of this interpretation is to help members quickly work out an acceptable twenty-four-hour schedule of AA living. This subject matter is founded on basic information from the book *Alcoholics Anonymous*.

All supplementary matter is based on practical experience from the lives of fellow alcoholics who have found peace of mind and contented sobriety by a planned way of spiritual life set forth in *Alcoholics Anonymous*.

We too often fail to realize the extent to which we are physically, mentally, and spiritually ill. Through ignorance we dwarf parts of our program to suit our distorted viewpoint.

It is obvious that much good can be accomplished by sharing with others the fund of knowledge that successful older members have gained by experience. The purpose of this introduction and the objective of this interpretation are toward that end.

As uncontrolled drinkers, few of us realized the danger of our position or how much alcoholism had damaged and deteriorated our minds and bodies. We didn't realize the full significance and effectiveness of our simple program without the help and cooperation of understanding members who had arrested their alcoholism.

Recovery through the AA program is simple. It needs little interpretation in itself. It will work if we live it. The barriers to success are ignorance of our illness, reservations, indifference, dishonesty, and brain damage.

AA is not religion. It is not accountable to organized religion, medicine, or psychology. AA has, however, drawn therapeutic virtues from these disciplines, molding them into a "design for living" by which we can live in contented sobriety and be restored to service and respect in society.

The AA program is designed for uncontrolled drinkers who sincerely desire sobriety and are willing to go to any length to get it. But the program invariably fails alcoholics who merely seek knowledge to control their drinking.

Stringent honesty is an absolute requirement of

rehabilitation. An urgent desire to get well and a belief in a Power greater than ourselves are also essential to success.

Spiritual concepts must be embraced, but these do not involve organized religion. Although we must believe in this *Higher Power*, it is our privilege to interpret it according to our understanding.*

The alcoholics who have recovered through the Alcoholics Anonymous fellowship internationally disprove the age-old conviction that all alcoholics are untrustworthy and destined to remain hopeless drunken sots. Hundreds of thousands have disproved this, and thousands of new alcoholics are daily proving that by living the AA philosophy, alcoholism can be arrested.

Daily sobriety is the simple aim of AA. But plain sobriety is not enough. We must acquire honesty, humility, appreciation, and kill self-centeredness to keep sober.

For those who are willing to accept the AA program as a means of recovery from alcoholism, we recommend a close study of *Alcoholics Anonymous*. Study it repeatedly.

Alcoholics Anonymous has all our answers; it was

---

*Read *Alcoholics Anonymous*, Chapter Four, pages 46-47.

written by alcoholics for alcoholics and is based on the trials and experiences of the first one hundred Alcoholics Anonymous members. They worked out a recovery program that has proved to be sound and effective in the lives of millions of alcoholics.

By using this as our textbook, regularly attending AA meetings, and referring to the interpretations of the Twelve Steps as we progress, we will lay a strong foundation upon which we can rehabilitate our lives.

We are not disturbed by the realization that strict adherence to this program demands perfection. We know perfection is impossible. We merely strive toward perfecting ourselves in a way of life that is necessary to bring contented sobriety, health, and sane behavior to alcoholics who wish to recover from the fatal and incurable illness, alcoholism.

AIDS TO CONTENTED SOBRIETY

Vital factors contributing to the long records of contented sobriety in the lives of thousands of AA members are their humility, honesty, faith, courage, gratitude, and service. The following AA definitions will be helpful in working out an acceptable understanding of these vital factors.

Humility

A true evaluation of conditions as they are; willingness to face facts; recognition of our alcoholic status; freedom from false pride and arrogance; understanding of the proper relationship between ourselves and a Higher Power, between ourselves and fellow human beings; acceptance and practice of this relationship throughout every twenty-four-hour period.

Honesty

Freedom from self-deception; trustworthiness in thought and action; sincerity in our desire to recover from alcoholism; willingness to admit a wrong; fairness in all our dealings with others; refusal to sneak that first drink.

Faith

Reliance, hope, and trust in the AA program; belief that we can recover as other members are doing and that practice of the Twelve Steps is necessary to happy, contented sobriety; willingness to draw on help from a Higher Power.

Courage

A quality of mind which enables us to deal with the problems and realities of life without reliance on alcohol; fortitude to endure the things we cannot change; a determination to stand our ground asking God's help with all issues, pleasant or otherwise, that might return us to drinking; fearlessness in the practice of faith, humility, honesty, and self-denial.

Gratitude

Gratitude continues the miracle of our sobriety. Gratitude is a healthy mental attitude; as we develop gratitude we enlarge our capacity for happiness, service, and contented sobriety. A lack of gratitude may lead to that first drink; gratitude and sobriety go hand in hand.

Service

Service to God and our fellow human beings is the key to AA success. Helping other alcoholics who need and want help gives us the tolerance and humility necessary to contented sobriety. Service combats self-centeredness. It reminds us of our powerlessness over alcohol. Intelligent, unselfish service is the lifeblood of the AA fellowship.

THE TWELVE STEPS*

STEP ONE. We admitted we were powerless over alcohol—that our lives had become unmanageable.

STEP TWO. Came to believe that a Power greater than ourselves could restore us to sanity.

STEP THREE. Made a decision to turn our will and our lives over to the care of God *as we understood Him.*

STEP FOUR. Made a searching and fearless moral inventory of ourselves.

STEP FIVE. Admitted to God, to ourselves, and to another human being the exact nature of our wrongs.

STEP SIX. Were entirely ready to have God remove all these defects of character.

STEP SEVEN. Humbly asked Him to remove our shortcomings.

STEP EIGHT. Made a list of all persons we had harmed, and became willing to make amends to them all.

*The Twelve Steps are taken from *Alcoholics Anonymous,* 3d ed., published by AA World Services, Inc., New York, NY, 59-60. Reprinted with permission of AA World Services, Inc. (see editor's note on the copyright page.)

STEP NINE. Made direct amends to such people wherever possible, except when to do so would injure them or others.

STEP TEN. Continued to take personal inventory and when we were wrong promptly admitted it.

STEP ELEVEN. Sought through prayer and meditation to improve our conscious contact with God *as we understood Him,* praying only for knowledge of His will for us and the power to carry that out.

STEP TWELVE. Having had a spiritual awakening as the result of these steps, we tried to carry this message to alcoholics, and to practice these principles in all our affairs.

STEP ONE

We admitted we were powerless over alcohol—that our lives had become unmanageable.

Men and women who are allergic to alcohol and who compulsively persist in drinking eventually become sick from a unique illness. This illness is known to medicine as alcoholism; it is unique in that it adversely affects us physically, mentally, and spiritually.

Step One briefly portrays the pathetic enigma of uncontrolled drinkers who have acquired this illness over which they are entirely powerless.

Drinkers of this type consider alcohol a physical requirement; they gradually increase its consumption at the expense of proper intake of nutritious foods. This practice induces physical and nervous disorders decidedly detrimental to their comfort and health.

The study of Step One will be largely devoted to

the physical illness of alcoholism.*

Few alcoholics have given their drinking problem much intelligent study. They reluctantly agree they must quit but keep right on drinking.

Severe hangovers make them realize that physical illness plays a part in their discomfort, but they resort to a little "hair off the dog that bit them" and continue into a new binge or finally taper off, suffering much physical and mental anguish.

The alcoholic lives in compulsive slavery. Alcohol is the only means that makes life bearable and quiets the alcoholic's jittery nerves. Existence under such circumstances soon makes the alcoholic's life unmanageable.

Correction of this condition is a serious problem of immediate concern. Recovery is possible for alcoholics who honestly want to stop drinking. "Unmanageable lives" and the physical illness induced by compulsive drinking can be arrested. We must have only a conscious need and desire for help.

The founders of Alcoholics Anonymous identified the physical factor as a part of their powerlessness over alcohol. This physical factor was given first

---

*Read "The Doctor's Opinion," page xxiii in *Alcoholics Anonymous*. For thirty-one daily health suggestions, read *Stools and Bottles*. Available through Hazelden Educational Materials.

consideration in their new recovery program. In twelve simple Steps they outlined a way of life for daily practice that restored them to physical health and contented sobriety. Daily practice was the key to their success.

By trial and error they designed a simple philosophy to arrest alcoholism. It embraced knowledge of many vital facts. Recovery is possible, but a cure cannot be effected. The man or woman who has become an alcoholic cannot become a controlled drinker. They have developed a serious illness, and their lowered physical and mental resistance is powerless. Control over alcohol is gone. Continued drinking now brings only physical illness and insane behavior. They are truly sick people.

Experience has proved that recovery from alcoholism is contingent on

1. Having a sincere desire to stop drinking.
2. Admitting and believing in our innermost hearts that we are powerless over alcohol.
3. Looking upon alcoholism as a fatal and incurable illness involving the body, mind, and spirit.
4. Considering ourselves as patients in AA for treatment.

5. Identifying alcohol as a poison rather than a beverage for us.
6. Making it our business to understand how alcohol affects us.
7. Realizing we are alcoholics.
8. Learning, practicing, and having faith in the Twelve Steps of the AA program.
9. Believing we can arrest our alcoholism, but we can never drink normally again.
10. Gaining a layperson's knowledge of how alcoholism affects our health and well-being.
11. Using this knowledge and understanding of our illness not only to gain sobriety but to guard against the danger of a return to drinking.
12. Doing this partially by keeping in our minds a mental picture of the unmanageable life alcohol demands from us and our powerlessness over it.

The layperson's view and understanding of alcoholism are simple ones based on known facts and backed up with his or her experiences and the knowledge gained from other alcoholics. The following discussion of alcoholism briefly covers the facts necessary to a beginner; the beginner's understanding will naturally increase as he or she makes the

Alcoholics Anonymous program a way of life.

Nature has provided each normal man and woman with a physical body designed to withstand the rigors of a strenuous daily life.

A healthy person can endure great hardships under most unfavorable circumstances as long as he or she receives oxygen, water, balanced nutrition, regular elimination, proper rest, and relaxation. The human tenacity to retain that spark of life is persistent as long as we follow these standards.

When one of these factors is permanently neglected, deficiencies will eventually occur, such as physical problems, nervous tension, and neurotic conditions. Our nervous systems will upset mental balance, and we will eventually die from lack of rest and nourishment.

Alcoholism stimulates such a condition and further complicates it by a daily intake of toxic poison—alcohol.

The bloodstream and body cells are first affected, then the brain, as we compulsively substitute the poison alcohol for the nutrition necessary to normal health.

This poison irritates the brain and finally breaks down nature's defensive barriers. Physical deterioration is sometimes rapid, but, in most alcoholics, addiction is acquired over a period of years, so it is only in the later stages of the illness that acute physical breakdown is apparent.

This breakdown is not apparent to the alcoholic, who is unable to visualize the hazards of his or her mental or physical condition. Alcoholism has gradually inhibited the alcoholic's power to discern between social and pathological drinking. A marked personality change, influenced chiefly by negative thinking, now drives the alcoholic to heavier drinking.

Friends and relatives become concerned over this change in personality. But, the alcoholic precludes self-criticism and becomes at odds with a normal environment.

Recovery from alcoholism, the illness which was responsible for our unmanageable lives, can only be accomplished when we stop drinking and return to a permanent, regular, balanced diet that completely eliminates alcohol. There is no shortcut, no substitute, no other way out for the alcoholic.

Controlled drinkers have no trouble conforming to this procedure, but alcoholics, who have lowered their physical resistance and exhausted their nervous system, should have medical help in starting rehabilitation.

Many members who ignore the importance of their physical well-being as an asset to recovery will fail to arrest their alcoholism. Some may recover, but they slow the process if they do not feel well physically.

We believe all alcoholics should be hospitalized upon request for help with the Alcoholics Anonymous program. This is not presently possible in all cases, so the members who cannot receive hospital care should consult a doctor who is skilled in the diagnosis and treatment of alcoholism.

The importance of this advice cannot be overemphasized. The alcoholic is a sick person who does not realize it and wishes to minimize his or her physical condition. This should not be allowed by the older members; they should point out the need for a complete physical checkup and see that the new member gets it.

Those who neglect the simple precaution of receiving ethical medical care are less apt to effect a speedy recovery from alcoholism.

The alcoholic whose life has become unmanageable from uncontrolled drinking is taking a serious step in identifying with our program and attempting to make it a way of life. The alcoholic's future security depends on the successful attainment of AA as a way of life. Alcoholics cannot allow impaired physical well-being to detract from chances of recovery; therefore, they must safeguard their health, as poor health may return them to drinking.

New members will benefit by investigating the various phases of alcoholism that apply to their cases; they must admit they are alcoholics and discuss their problems with older members who are always willing to offer advice and help.

Learn to see in alcoholism a diseased condition of the nervous system due to the excessive use of alcohol. Reflect upon your powerlessness over this sickness. Learn a number of the tests in the medical and psychological field that identify alcoholics. Admit you "can't take it." Consider your inability to take it or leave it alone; remember your inability to leave alcohol alone in the face of impending disaster. If you drink, it definitely marks you as an alcoholic. The necessity of a drink "the morning after" is common to most alcoholics. There are many other identifications of the alcoholic; make it your business to learn some of them.

The founders of Alcoholics Anonymous understood that members have to realize their physical illness and receive medical help before they can concentrate on the spiritual requirements necessary in recovery. Physical health is a necessity, but it is only the first step in recovery from our alcoholic illness.

SUMMARIZATION. Recovery from alcoholism first involves a layperson's knowledge of this illness and a conscious need for its treatment. There is no mystery about it. Addiction to alcohol has set up a poisoning within our bodies. Compulsive drinking, over which we are powerless, naturally follows. Our lives become unmanageable. The First Step of recovery is to recognize our alcoholism and admit our physical illness.

WHY DOES THIS HELP? It makes us honest in evaluating our true physical condition. It makes us humble and willing to stop alcoholic rationalization. It awakens us to our need for hospitalization before entering AA and for medical care afterwards.

WHY ARE WE SICK? CAN WE BE CURED? Real alcoholics are sick from poisoning acquired by substituting alcohol for food and rest. Physical health can be restored, but no cure will permit us to become controlled drinkers.

TREATMENT. Admitting our alcoholism. Willingness to accept medical treatment. Proper diet and relaxation. Belief we can recover. Daily practice of our AA program.

Drugs

Occasionally, some of us have resorted to drugs for physical comfort or to induce sleep. This practice is *out* for all alcoholics, except those rare cases where an ethical medical practitioner, skilled in the treatment of alcoholism, prescribes and supervises such treatment.

We live the AA program to develop normal, well-integrated personalities that exclude the use of the narcotic, alcohol. Drugs prevent this change in personality. They warp our thinking. They too quickly become a substitute for alcohol and are decidedly habit forming for most of us.

STEP TWO

Came to believe that a Power greater than ourselves could restore us to sanity.[*]

Step Two deals with mental illness. However intelligent we may have been in other respects, wherever alcohol has been involved, we have been strangely insane. It's strong language, but isn't it true?[**]

No alcoholic acts sanely while drinking. Chronic poisoning from alcohol results in compulsive drinking and insane behavior. Willpower is not a factor in recovery until the compulsion has been removed. Since reservations defeat any honest attempt to stop drinking, we find it necessary to recognize our mental instability. Dodging the truth only results in distorted thinking and opposition to help from a Power greater than ourselves.

[*]Before studying Step Two, read pages 36-39 of *Alcoholics Anonymous*.
[**]Read page 33 in *Twelve Steps and Twelve Traditions* (New York, A.A. World Services, Inc., 1953). Available through Hazelden Educational Materials, Center City, MN.

Those of us who have had an honest desire to recover from the mental sickness that alcoholism has imposed upon us have successfully used this Power. Our sick personalities find a sure source of power and healing in *God, as we understand Him.* God renews our minds and straightens our thinking.

Step Two opens a vista of new hope, when based on willingness and faith. What we call this Power is a matter of choice. Call It what we will. Naming It is unimportant. The important thing is that we believe in It, that we use It to restore us to mental health and fitness.

Faith in a Higher Power is a basic law of recovery. It is always evident in the lives of successful members. What they have done, we can do. By practicing the Twelve Steps we gain a conscious contact with this Power to live in contented sobriety.

Mental handicaps stand between us and recovery. Our lack of self-criticism defeats an honest evaluation of our alcoholism. Use of the word *sanity* offends our false pride. We admit our illness but rebel against questions of mental soundness. This partial acceptance is a hazard to our sobriety. We benefit most from accepting Step Two with no reservations.

As a beginner, you will avoid confusion in the interpretation of this Step if you approach it with a sincere desire for the accepted AA meaning. Remind yourself that you are making the AA recovery program your way of life because it is essential to your recovery from alcoholism. Your life depends on this program along with your mental and physical well-being, your happiness, and the security of your home—your very life. It might be suicidal to disagree with any part of it, so resolve to be open-minded and accept the Twelve Steps in their entirety.

Some members have eventually arrived at the true meaning of Step Two by temporarily rephrasing it to read, "Came to believe that a Power greater than ourselves could restore us to sane behavior."

The truth is most members have acted insane only during periods of intoxication. This is common practice for all drinkers who get "tight," but to the alcoholic who shortens the intervals between periods of intoxication and finally merges them into one long "drunk," it becomes a serious matter. Insane behavior because of an evening's drinking is generally excused, but when carried on for weeks and months that lengthen into years, it becomes a pattern that is fixed in the brain.

We cannot overlook the harmful effect of the prolonged use of alcohol or its unhealthy mental condition which results in complacent disregard of sane thought or normal behavior. Using alcoholics cannot control their impulses; they lack mental coordination. Continued use of alcohol damages the brain and sometimes causes insanity.

Signs of such injury seem to exist in all alcoholics in proportion to their physical resistance to alcohol poisoning and to the length of time involved in abnormal drinking.

Alcoholics who cling to the illusion that they exercise sanity in their drinking are invited to prove their case against the accepted definition of insanity.

A simple definition of insanity is a disorder of behavior that occurs when the body impulses no longer find in the brain a coordinating center for the conditioning of behavior. When this condition arises, the person's behavior is unpredictable and he or she becomes legally insane.

The conduct of the uncontrolled drinker who has become alcoholic is likewise unpredictable. The alcoholic's friends and relatives take on long faces as alcoholism perverts the power of reason, dulls talent, and limits self-preservation, making the alcoholic irresponsible and a menace to society.

How is the alcoholic to account for the insane impulse that prompts him or her to reach for that first drink that starts another binge?

Is it a sane act? Is the alcoholic obsessed? Is it the result of irrational thinking? Does it involve thinking? Does sanity in an alcoholic imply the power to accept or reject that first drink?

We think it does; we do not believe the alcoholic can help him- or herself. We believe and know from experience that a Power greater than ourselves can remove this obsession, straighten the twisted thinking, and restore the alcoholic to sane thought and behavior.

Those who disapprove of the word *sanity* in Step Two are usually alcoholics who have been fortunate enough to escape the more serious aspects of alcoholism. They reason they were perfectly normal between drinking bouts.*

Alcoholics who did themselves no serious damage during their drinking careers should find solace in that fact. They should take a broad view of the insanity of alcoholism, since most of us were surely deranged over varying periods of time.

We must also remember in the progressive development of alcoholism the power of reasoning is slowly deteriorated. This encourages deception over our real mental health and fitness; it breeds a superior feeling of false security.

---

*Read pages 36-43 in *Alcoholics Anonymous*.

Evidence to support this fact is found in the following danger symptoms commonly seen in alcoholics:

1. Taking that first drink with the idea that "this time I'll control it."
2. The continued use of alcohol and reliance upon it for physical and mental power to meet our daily responsibilities.
3. The necessity of the drink "the morning after."
4. Our inability to be self-critical of the sanity of our behavior over prolonged years of drinking—our refusal to consider the harm we have done to ourselves and others.
5. The faith we placed in childish excuses for our drinking and the stupid alibis we thought we were getting away with.
6. The reckless abandon we displayed in drunken driving—the argument that we drive better while drunk than while sober, and our resentment toward those who differed from this opinion.
7. The critical physical condition we reach and the continued suffering we endure from uncontrolled drinking.
8. The financial risks taken—the shame, sorrow, and often poverty that we inflict upon our families.

9. The asinine resentments that clogged our minds. Our loss of responsibility. Getting ourselves drunk to spite or injure others. The erroneous assumption that we can "take it or leave it alone." Our unnecessary squandering of money.

10. Blackouts.

11. Contemplated or attempted suicide.

These are a few symptoms, common to alcoholics, that indicate mental illness. They justify our deduction that alcohol, in large or small doses, has become a poison that induces unpredictable behavior and limits mental coordination.

There is no point in deceiving ourselves over the fate of the alcoholic who continues to use alcohol. There are just two escapes from drinking: one is insanity; the other is alcoholic death. The purpose of the AA program as a way of life is to avoid both by arresting the illness, alcoholism.

As alcoholics we cannot undo our past behavior; we can, however, use the knowledge of our escape from insanity and alcoholic death as an incentive to contact God for help in keeping us from future drinking.

It is now our privilege to draw on the help of a

Power greater than ourselves to arrest our alcoholism. The alcoholic record of our past life is not the basis that our future will be judged on. We have a new page before us; we are invited to "write our own ticket." Sobriety, sanity, security, and peace of mind are within our reach.

The future, with the AA program as our way of life, will bring us sane, useful, happy lives. We have learned our lesson: alcohol is poison that causes mental illness and insane behavior.

Surely, with this knowledge, we can never lay claim to sanity if we again take that first drink.

MENTAL DRUNKENNESS

In spite of all knowledge some of us willfully continue in self-centeredness. We ignore our mental illness. Alcoholic thinking displaces humility, and we return to physical drunkenness through lack of spiritual growth and understanding.

Looking at our failure, we discover we have built up resentment, self-pity, and physical or mental exhaustion, and our faith in a Power greater than ourselves was inadequate.

We should never forget physical drunkenness is always preceded by mental binges that end in spiritual blackouts. They leave us blind and helpless, insulating us from the Power that our sanity and sobriety depend on. We can detect them if we will observe the danger signals so apparent during the buildup of the mental binge.

SUMMARIZATION. Mental illness is understandable when we first concede our physical illness. Sick bodies do not house healthy minds. As alcoholics, we cannot think or act sanely while drinking or sobering up. Our wills work subject to alcoholic poisoning. Remove the poisoning and free will is restored. It is not dependable, however, so we turn it over to God for help. These are the basic recovery fundamentals of Step Two.

SYMPTOMS OF MENTAL ILLNESS. Continued drinking. Blackouts. Mental drunkenness. Avoiding self-criticism. Emotional instability. Stinking thinking. Deep resentments. Fits of anger. Planned or attempted suicide. Delusions.

TREATMENT. Honest evaluation of our sick personalities and of the inadequacy of the human will to remedy them. Conscious need for treatment. Willingness to recover from our illness. Belief that a Power greater than ourselves can restore us to sane thought and behavior. Dependence upon a Higher Power for recovery from our mental illness.

RECOVERY. We attain spiritual strength, understanding, humility, emotional stability, peace of mind, and contented sobriety.

STEP THREE

*Made a decision to turn our will and our
lives over to the care of God*
as we understood Him.

Step Three identifies the spiritual illness of alcoholism and suggests a simple, effective remedy. Success with this or other Steps is not a matter of chance but of right thought and motive practiced daily.

Knowledge and treatment of our physical and mental health are vitally important to alcoholics, but lasting, contented sobriety is maintained only by surrender of our lives and will to God as we understand Him.

The first three Steps are a composite AA package. Conceived of meditation and experience, they are a basic recovery prescription. Taken with proper timing and in correct proportion they immediately arrest our alcoholic illness. These Steps complement each other, but they fail to work if any of them are omitted.

Steps One and Two are the premise upon which we decide to surrender our alcoholic lives to God. Step Three calls for this decision. Honesty, faith, and prayer spark our success.

A complete knowledge of the physical, mental, and spiritual injury we have suffered at the hands of "John Barleycorn" is indispensable to the honest, far-reaching decision we wish to make. Deliberation born of necessity and a desperate need for help will inspire us to seek our understanding of God.

Our great need is loss of self-centeredness and alcoholic obsession. AA pioneers discovered their answers to these problems as they developed spiritual understanding and relied upon God's help for recovery. Each of us has the same possibilities if we are honest, humble, and willing enough to work them out.

Step Three offers no compromise for reservation or delay. It calls for a decision, here and now. How we surrender our alcoholic personality defects to God is of no immediate concern. The important point is our willingness to try. Faith in practice of the Twelve Steps opens the way to understanding of God and provides ways of giving our lives to Him.

When we have made this crucial decision, our attitude changes rapidly from negative to wholesome, constructive thinking. We lose our uncertainty and fear. Strife and rebellion disappear. Somehow, we seem to gain a vague understanding of God's will for us. This understanding may be small, but it is all we need to start with. It comes slowly at first.

Members who have accepted and practiced Step Three know the value of turning the defects of their alcoholic lives over to the care of God as they understand Him. Faith in His help and willingness to try AA spiritual practices will convert our weaknesses to great spiritual strength and understanding. Contented sobriety, the central purpose in our lives, is not earned without self-sacrifice and God's help.

If fear of public opinion, spiritual bias, or hypocritical ideas stand in our way, we learn to overcome them. We have no other choice. It is a small price to pay for life and sanity, particularly when we learn our prejudice is but preconceived judgment inspired by ill health, ignorance, and false pride.

Public opinion is for, not against, us. Spiritual bias is but self-will that does not yield to reason. Trying to understand God's will for us is not hypocritical. It is a basic recovery principle for alcoholics. It never fails those who sincerely use it.

AA is an anonymous fellowship that will shield us from publicity, a place where we escape the doom of alcoholic death by life on a spiritual basis.* The public's only knowledge of our lives is that we no longer drink. They did not approve of our drinking, but they honor and receive us when we stop. This is plain, unmistakable evidence of spiritual progress.

After making our decision to live on a moral, spiritual basis, many perplexities arise. How are we to understand God? How are we to submit our will and our lives to Him?

We are advised the AA program is simple, and we should keep it as simple as possible. Yet in Step Three we are confronted with the age-old mystery of humankind's relativity to God. Our natural inclination is to duck the issue entirely. Surely there must be some easier way out. There is. Given a chance, our alcoholic minds will find it. It leads back to drinking.

We know what should be done about this matter, but we are not being honest with ourselves when we refuse to seek an understanding of God or to draw upon His help and power. We still reason through alcoholic thinking. It is hard to surrender the rationalization and alibis of our alcoholic personalities. Also while seeking a tangible God we miss the service that leads to Him.

---

*Read pages 44-45 of *Alcoholics Anonymous*.

After groping around in the murky fog of rebellion, stinking thinking, and despair, we will come up with our answers. Honest and sincere as we try to make them, they are usually most confusing. When we overlook the fact that we are ill, it is easy to see only moral offense in our conduct and decide religion is the answer to our problems. But those of us who have tried to exclude AA generally end up drunk.

We should not confuse organized religion with AA. We can keep our religion separate and not substitute it for AA philosophy. Honest clergy members expedite spiritual attainment but usually lack understanding of the physical and mental illness of alcoholism. If your priest, minister, or rabbi is interested in AA, he or she can undoubtedly help you. Regardless of such support, join an AA group.

Obviously, religious creeds must be dealt with outside of AA. Our concept of God as we understand Him and our belief in a Higher Power that can restore spiritual health are all our program requires. We find it most adequate.

A great barrier in finding God is impatience. We soon learn spiritual attainment must be earned. Understanding of God constantly enlarges so we never reach perfection.

Since this is no overnight process, we suggest thought and prayer in the matter. At the start we make separate approaches to surrendering our willful lives and reaching our concept of God. By first deciding what isolates us from Him we reach a spiritual awakening as we eliminate these isolating factors or character defects.

We deal with God in the abstract; thus our contacts must be on a mental plane. We believe acts of drunkenness, dishonesty, envy, self-pity, spite, hatred, resentment, malice, and injustice injure us; they are the acts of depraved people in the eyes of society and are opposed to all spiritual virtues known to AA members who are spiritually awakened.

If this is true and we can accept it, as a majority of our membership have, then the matter of what we turn over to God's care is no longer a problem. We find all of these traits in our unmanageable alcoholic lives. If these are spiritual debits, most of us have drunk ourselves into spiritual bankruptcy.

Step Three should not confuse us. It calls for a decision to correct our character defects under spiritual supervision. The common cause of failure is time and effort spent in visualizing God or vaguely trying to reach Him before we make a decision to surrender and change our insane, unmanageable lives.

We demand maturity without the pains of experience and growth. This is both unreasonable and impossible. By such method we would have a program of three Steps, rather than twelve. It is the practice of Steps Four through Twelve that teaches us our understanding of God. This understanding starts with blind faith; through conviction it steadily grows into conscious contact with God—personal contact. *Spiritual growth is our goal.* We are wise to avoid all concepts of God opposed to that goal.

Lack of faith arrests our progress. Procrastination and skepticism are enemies of spiritual attainment. Skepticism demands evidence of God's help. Procrastination prevents it. Faith, willingness, and prayer overcome all obstacles and provide ample evidence of His help in our happy, sober lives.

We usually experience our best understanding of God when we humbly admit our alcoholic illness and sincerely lose ourselves in the AA way of life. Friendly acts of service, forgiveness, and amends help our understanding.

God speaks to us in as many ways as we find to contact Him. His answers, abstract as they may be, are detected in mind, emotion, and in the new conscience we have developed. We are inspired in accordance with our thought and conduct, either with feelings of faith, accomplishment, and serenity, or with confusion, self-pity, and fear.

Few alcoholics need introduction to the idea of a Divine Being. Most of us were taught this in our youth. We have all seen evidence of a Power greater than ourselves in our well-regulated world of seasons, day and night, heat and moisture, human reproduction, and love and tolerance.

Most of us have appreciated the perfection of the universe, the animation of living things, the action of the human mind, and the power of love. These things all seem to denote a dynamic life force that surges through everything around us. This force appears to direct all things harmoniously but irresistibly toward a natural, definite, useful conclusion.

Is it hard to recognize in this life force a Power greater than ourselves:? Do we not sense Its creative energy, intelligence, and power? Are human beings not weak and unimportant apart from God's power?

Our founders discovered, by trial and error, that spiritual contact with God as they understood Him was the alcoholic's only assurance of a normal, sober life.

Self-preservation urges that we find this companionship and try to understand God's help.

Understanding comes slowly from practice of the Twelve Steps. From simple acts, such as:

1. Humbly admitting our alcoholism. Desiring to stop drinking and treat our illness.
2. Honest effort to lose alcoholic skepticism. Faith in God and the AA program.
3. Making a decision to live as free as possible of mental binges.
4. Identifying character defects that isolate us from contented sobriety.
5. Submitting these defects in prayer to God for removal.
6. Honestly living each Step to establish a conscious contact with Him.
7. Prayer without resentment in our hearts.
8. Studying the Big Book for understanding to improve our conscience. Forgiving others.
9. Dealing in right motives, fair treatment.
10. Acting with kindness and sanity in our business and home life.
11. Being honest and appreciative, helping others, showing tolerance.
12. Belief in our spiritual potential. Willingness to find God in developing it.

The important element is our willingness to *try*. Every alcoholic has spiritual possibilities. We must learn to bring them out, to form convictions, and to let them grow.

When it is possible, we should take our spouses or close relatives into our confidence as we attempt to carry out this Step. We have found great strength, and help comes to members who have the confidence and cooperation of those close to them. If family members are not cooperative, we must work it out alone.

We should avoid the common mistake of confusing our minds with anxious thoughts regarding the time and manner God will manifest Himself to us. Our understanding will come gradually as we earn and develop it.

It is uncommon for a member to have a drastic spiritual upheaval. Spiritual awakening or experience comes slowly, and often in strange ways. It does come, however, but so naturally we often fail to recognize it.

Our job is to be ready and willing for these experiences, find incentive in the examples of fellow members who are living the AA program, be open-minded in our endeavor to understand God and realize that it is not made up of one big accomplishment but gained bit by bit, and remember our inspiration will be influenced by our attitude and action.* The active members who take the program

---

*Our recovery from alcoholism is dependent on humility, honesty, faith in God, appreciation, and service to other alcoholics.

seriously are slowly but surely laying the groundwork for close personal contacts with God—by applying it in their home life, in their business, and in the treatment of new members; by admitting wrongs; and by making amends.

Quiet periods of relaxation and prayer are necessary to achieve this Step. The alcoholic should also keep in mind the value of relaxation aside from prayer. We should not overlook the fact that all alcoholics are of restless disposition, that restlessness and tension are a part of our trouble, that we once appeased this condition with alcohol, and that we now seek to correct it under God's supervision.

Alcoholics must learn to relax when they become upset, angry, impatient, resentful, bored, or exhausted.

Relaxation helps us maintain physical, mental, and spiritual balance. It aids clear thinking which keeps us out of the "driver's seat." It permits conscious contact with God—our only hope for recovery from alcoholism.

We regard the outcome of this Step in complete confidence, as we know from the example of other members that God's will can be understood and that our understanding of His care will give us new personalities that exclude alcohol—personalities that happily relate us to God, to a conventional world, and to others.

SUMMARIZATION. The confusing ills of alcoholism need no longer frustrate the alcoholic who wants to get well. Steps One and Two clearly reveal alcoholism as a sickness—a fatal, incurable malady.

Chronic alcohol poisoning induced by addiction to alcohol accounts for our physical and mental illness. This illness is the premise that we base our decision on—to seek God's help for recovery.

Spiritual illness loses its mystery and vagueness when we concede the anesthetic role alcohol has played in our lives. It explains the mental paralysis and moral deviations associated with compulsive drinking. We come to know that self-pity, fear, intolerance, resentment, belligerency, vindictiveness, and dishonesty have insulated us from God. They have callused our consciences. They have bred spiritual illness.

Step Three confuses us only when we reverse its suggested application. The Step has three parts: first, a decision; second, we try to determine what constitutes our will and our life; and third, we seek an understanding of God by placing our will and our life in His care.

TREATMENT. We stop playing God. We surrender our self-centeredness to Him. We relax. We avoid confusing AA with religion. We do not try to define

God. We recognize and attempt to develop our spiritual possibilities. We seek a personal contact with God, practicing thought and action with moral values that help us develop a better conscience. We plan and try to live daily lives that embrace sobriety, faith, honesty, prayer, tolerance, forgiveness, service to others, and amends where they should be made.

Spiritual upheavals and overnight personality changes are not for most of us. We come to know God from living the Twelve Steps. If we wish to have God's help in our hour of need, let's get out our pencils and paper now and list the things that Step Four identifies as barriers to His help in our recovery from alcoholism.

STEP FOUR

*Made a searching and fearless moral
inventory of ourselves.*

The purpose of taking a moral inventory is to expose
the harmful character traits of our alcoholic personalities and to eliminate them from the new personalities with the help of the Alcoholics Anonymous
program as a way of life we now propose to develop.

The AA use of the term *personality* deals with the
development of new character traits necessary to our
recovery from alcoholism. It has no relation to
personal magnetism emanating from physical health,
beauty, or charm.

We gauge AA personality by AA maturity that is
evidenced by such qualities as: strength and understanding from a Power greater than ourselves, surrender of self-centeredness, the practice of honesty,
humility, gratitude, forgiveness, promptness in admitting wrongs, making amends, service to others,
and the example of a happy, sober life.

Before we can hope to develop the qualities that will create desirable AA personalities, we must discover the causes for our powerlessness over alcohol; we wish to know why we have been at war with ourselves; we propose to reveal and to study the limitations that alcoholism has placed upon our lives.

We hope to transcend our alcoholic limitations, to straighten our unmanageable lives, so we check our alcoholic personalities. "First, we searched out the flaws in our make-up which caused our failure."[*]

The gravity of our drinking problem is deep-seated; it involves self-centered habits, physical health, emotions, and misconceptions acquired over a period of years. They have sapped our mental powers, weakened our physical resistance, and have sponsored irrational thought and action. This has caused us extreme mental and physical hardship and brought anxiety and suffering to others.

Arresting our alcoholism is not possible until we have knowledge of our defects; therefore, we take definite steps toward correction of our physical, mental, and spiritual disability. We do this when we make a searching and fearless moral inventory of ourselves; when we do it in a thorough, businesslike

---

[*]Read pages 63 (bottom) through 64 of *Alcoholics Anonymous*.

way; and when we reasonably excuse other people and truly expose our own faults.

The beginner cannot fail to be impressed with the array of flaws he or she will uncover and will wish to correct. The caution to be observed in taking this Step is *few of us are ready and willing to surrender all our defects.* We wish to cherish a few, and by this procedure we encounter future trouble in the form of partial rehabilitation which is not the plan of the AA recovery program.

This Step calls for a *thorough inventory;* our program is not in accord with halfway measures or efforts; full rehabilitation is our objective. Reservations defeat this purpose. They take the contentment out of sobriety. Let's be wise and employ the inventory 100 percent.

A moral inventory of a lifetime of drinking is not quickly recorded, nor is it a record that can be simply stated. We find many complexities that require study and meditation. It must be honest, sincere, and thorough. To be effective it must be a written inventory as it will later be checked against and often referred to. The mental self-appraisal is merely a supplement to the written inventory. It is necessary but not sufficient in itself.

Experience has taught us this Step should be

started at once and left open for future reference, so during the process of our mental and spiritual cleanup we can add new items that present themselves.

The brief discussion of a few imperfections that appears in this book is entirely inadequate, compared to the thought and time you will need in applying this Step to your alcoholic problem.

We can refer to the bottom of page 63 through the end of Chapter Five in *Alcoholics Anonymous* for a detailed discussion of Step Four. From these pages you will learn the manner that AA founders advocated for working out our inventories.

You will discover various manifestations of self-centeredness are undoubtedly the root of your trouble, and some of these manifestations present themselves in the form of resentment, dishonesty, self-pity, jealousy, criticism, intolerance, fear, and anger.

RESENTMENT

Resentment is common among all alcoholics. We are never safe from it and, as intangible as it may seem, it does pay off in material ways with destructive force and energy. Resentment is dynamite to the alcoholic.

In studying *Alcoholics Anonymous*, we are reminded "resentment is the 'number one' offender. It destroys more alcoholics than anything else. From it stem all forms of spiritual disease, for we have been not only mentally and physically ill, we have been spiritually sick."[*] Resentment is pure mental drunkenness. We must treat it mentally and spiritually to remain physically dry.

". . . In dealing with resentments, we set them on paper. We listed people, institutions or principles with whom we were angry. We asked ourselves why we were angry. In most cases it was found that our self-esteem, our pocketbooks, our ambitions, our personal relationships (including sex) were hurt or threatened. So we were sore. We were 'burned up.'"[**]

Make up your grudge list, decide who is enclosed in your circle of hatred, and determine why you hold them there. Has your life been any happier because of this resentment? Were they really the offenders?

The founders of Alcoholics Anonymous answer the question with the definite statement: "It is plain that a life which includes deep resentment leads only to

---

[*] Read *Alcoholics Anonymous*, Chapter Five, page 64. See *Stools and Bottles*, pages 80-81.
[**] *Alcoholics Anonymous*, Chapter Five, pages 64-65.

futility and unhappiness. To the precise extent that we permit these, do we squander the hours that might have been worth while."*

They explain that resentment dwarfs the maintenance and growth of spiritual experience which is the only hope of the alcoholic.

DISHONESTY

"Those who do not recover are people who cannot or will not completely give themselves to this simple program, usually men and women who are constitutionally incapable of being honest with themselves."**

Dishonesty requires little further comment. It has no place in our program. It must be eliminated if we are to succeed at all.

Honesty with yourself, God, and other people is the keystone in the AA bridge that spans the alcoholic chasm to permanent, happy sobriety.

Without honesty the AA program would become an inconsistent, hypocritical way of life. It would become negative and antagonistic to recovery. The practice of dishonesty in any form helps to tear down

---

Alcoholics Anonymous, Chapter Five, page 66.
**Alcoholics Anonymous*, Chapter Five, page 58.

the alcoholic's defense against that first drink which the alcoholic will eventually take if he or she cannot be honest.

CRITICISM

Criticism, a form of negative judgment, is absolutely out of our fellowship picture. It is a black sheep in the AA family, a malicious carrier of strife and rebellion. It deprives us of peace of mind and contented sobriety.

Well-meaning advice can be most helpful because of its sincerity.

Criticism is viciously opposed to the AA personalities we are trying to develop. It is not a gesture of cooperation indicating friendly interest, but rather a destructive force that breeds self-pity, jealousy, resentment, and ill will.

The common interest of the AA program is sobriety. Criticism has no place in helping either an individual or a group to gain or maintain sobriety.

Faultfinding and gossip will destroy the results of constructive AA efforts. They serve no good purpose and should be controlled with tolerance and understanding, curbing our tendencies toward criticism.

If you must deal in criticism, confine your practice to self-criticism.

SELF-PITY

Self-pity is not generally regarded by alcoholics as a particularly harmful emotion. We have all indulged in varied forms of self-pity, the most common being the type experienced while enduring the tortures of a hangover. Other forms of self-pity involve resentment and hatred brought on by real or fancied wrongs, by acts of God, by ill luck or disease.

Self-pity is often outright rebellion against circumstances of our own making when we feel sorry for ourselves and assume negative attitudes toward life.

It is not until we see in this emotion evidence of resentment and until we realize that it gives us the wrong attitude toward life and toward those with whom we associate, that we understand the necessity for its elimination.

We alcoholics free ourselves from all forms of resentment; our happiness in life depends on our attitudes and service toward others. We cannot afford to subject ourselves to self-pity because of its relationship to resentment and inferiority. Self-pity retards our recovery from alcoholism by closing our minds to the wholesome, helpful opportunities around us; it promotes self-centered thinking that should be directed toward understanding God and establishing an intimate relationship with Him.

Emotional maturity and AA growth are stunted by self-pity. This extreme form of self-centeredness lacks faith and opposes spiritual growth. We seek God's help to treat this most serious character defect.

TREATMENT. Recognize self-pity. Pray to lose this defect. Cultivate appreciation of our sobriety. Thank God for it. Help another alcoholic. Thus we develop new spiritual strength that supplants fear and dependency. Thus we eliminate self-pity.

JEALOUSY

Few, if any, men or women escape this emotional monstrosity. Jealousy's width and length are fear and self-pity. Its depth is anger, resentment, and frustration.

Jealousy of another's good standing, personality, talent, or personal possessions can prey upon the human mind until, like a malignant cancer, it injures or destroys.

The beginner who takes the time to analyze jealousy finds in it a combination of all his or her pet imperfections. You are advised to make this analysis and acquaint yourself with this harmful form of mental drunkenness.

Search for "blind spots" that lead alcoholics back to compulsive drinking.

A close inspection will show an astounding array of moral defects. They may appear in mild or passive form, yet they are all there: self-pity, resentment, intolerance, dishonesty, criticism, suspicion, anger. From this inspection we learn that fear and frustration bind them all together.

It is well to avoid this compound emotion which can so easily jeopardize a member's mental health and lead him or her into resentment, bitter hatred, and drunkenness.

INTOLERANCE

Lack of tolerance has much to do with that first drink which under certain circumstances the alcoholic is unable to resist.

This condition existed when physical distress was experienced, when the realities of life became too demanding on our time and energy, when mental tension was great, when resentment at home or in business became unbearable, when business was poor, when we became fatigued through overactivity, or when we were faced with other distracting circumstances. We felt that conditions had reached a breaking point; we became intolerant of them, so we got drunk.

We should never forget the intolerable hangovers, the despair of compulsive drinking, or God's help in its removal. We need more help with new problems. Do not expect God to eliminate them overnight. The practice of tolerance is a part of recovery. It aids spiritual progress and helps us control our emotions. It nurtures contented sobriety.

Evidence of intolerance in a member is not a good sign. It shows lack of equilibrium and indicates symptoms of an unstable mental and spiritual status. Our attitude of tolerance, where it should reasonably be expected, reflects our understanding and practice of the AA philosophy as a way of life.

Alcoholics have consistently poached on the tolerance of humankind. They have much to amend in this respect and should reverse their field at once by showing consideration where it is due.

We do not believe tolerance of improper situations makes good sense. God gave us intelligence to determine between good and bad; therefore, we find as much harm in being tolerant of wrong thought or action as we find in intolerance of the right things.

Discretion in the use of tolerance is necessary, but if we are practicing the AA program as a way of life we will find ourselves compromising with persons whom we have long been intolerant of. Tolerance toward both new and old members who are sincerely trying to live this program is essential to our recovery from alcoholism. If they are honestly trying to make AA their way of life, we owe them our help.

It is not wise to become intolerant of conditions that we cannot change; the AA program advises us to gain an understanding of God's will. The condition that cannot be changed may be against the will of God. We should not view it with intolerance, but rather direct our time and energy in helpful constructive activity where satisfactory results are possible.

God grant us the serenity to accept the things we cannot change, courage to change the things we can, and wisdom to know the difference.

FEAR

The tendency of alcoholics to discount fear as contributing to alcoholism often causes newcomers to underrate its importance to their inventories. They erroneously associate fear with cowardice and want no part of it. Yet fear had much to do with their drinking, and full knowledge of it is essential to their recovery.

It is an emotion that has a definite place in the lives of all human beings. Primitive humans could not have survived without it. Experience made them afraid of dangerous or destructive things which they were powerless over, and fear then supplied the extra energy needed to avoid or escape bad circumstances.

When used for actual purposes of self-preservation, fear gives us the caution and the discretion necessary for requirements of everyday living. Fear prompts us to take safe procedures and to protect our families against poverty and disease. Under its impulse, we gain energy to build homes, to work, to face reality, and to assume responsibility.

As alcoholics, we have used a few of fear's positive qualities, but we have primarily utilized the negative aspects, specializing in anxiety, dread, worry, uncertainty, and apprehension of harm or evil that always seemed just around the corner. Urged by fear of hangovers and alcoholic insomnia, we hid liquor all over our homes. Fear of truth filled us with dread and uncertainty. Anxiety constantly beset our efforts to conceal addiction, to uphold our lies, to dodge our creditors. Fear of domination, public opinion, loss of home, and finances allowed no peace of mind.

The negative elements of fear belong in our inventories. On page 65, Chapter Five, of *Alcoholics*

Anonymous, we find examples of fear in our lives and a way to classify them. Part of our personality change centers around our understanding and treatment of this emotion.

The AA program is not founded upon fear. It is a spiritual way of life based on *Power* other than our own, on faith in a *Power greater than ourselves* to overcome fear and other defects of our alcoholic personalities. We have seen members try to find contented sobriety basing their attempt on self-education motivated by the fear of alcohol. They do not stay sober long. We have known them to try to protect themselves from drinking by total absence from bars and nightclubs under the assumption that they would be sorely tempted by such environment. From their experience we believe that such abnormal worry indicates a half-hearted attempt at the program and is in reality an unacknowledged desire to drink again.

Alcoholics Anonymous states, "In our belief any scheme of combating alcoholism which proposes to shield the sick man from temptation is doomed to failure. If the alcoholic tries to shield himself he may succeed for a time, but he usually winds up with a bigger explosion than ever. We have tried these methods. These attempts to do the impossible have always failed.

"So our rule is not to avoid a place where there is drinking *if we have a legitimate reason for being there.* . Go or stay away, whichever seems best. But be sure you are on solid spiritual ground before you start and that your motive in going is thoroughly good."*

Being on spiritual ground is the important thing, but we must not overlook the fact that we have a definite part to play. God can help us only if we are willing and trying to get well. The realization that temptation will always be present and that we never have successfully avoided it before should bring us close to God for help. We have no knowledge of how or when the urge to drink will come. We know it will, however, and we cannot wait until it is upon us. We must prepare ourselves with faith and prayer for our hour of need.

Steps One and Two suggest we come to an understanding of all our alcoholic problems. We are never to forget our powerlessness over alcohol and the insane behavior and unmanageable living it brings. Nature backs up this theory with dreams of drinking. Dreams that are so realistic they fill us with genuine

---

*Read pages 101-102, Chapter Seven, in *Alcoholics Anonymous*.

remorse and further our determination to gain contented sobriety.

We must admit we are alcoholic; it is good for us to do so. All members should strive to cultivate an honest, realistic evaluation of what alcohol does to them as partial insurance against a possible return to drinking. This does not imply the use of fear, but rather of intelligence to avoid further alcohol addiction. We are not afraid of alcohol. Alcohol can be all around us without harmful effects if our "spiritual ground" is right and we are on a twenty-four-hour practice of our philosophy. We should, however, be afraid to drink it, as we would be afraid of any other poison.

Thus we fortify our minds with prayer and with the mental resources God has given us. Intelligent use of mental pictures, based on knowledge of our alcoholic status, is invaluable to our recovery from alcoholism. We do not rebel against the fact we cannot drink or use other poisons. Contented sobriety will come easier when we have learned to take alcohol out of the beverage classification and place it where it rightfully belongs for us—among the poisons.

Members who are unable to overcome their fear by practice of the AA program should consult their doctors or psychiatrists who will probably be able to help them. Such aid plus help from our program usually straightens them out and makes contented sobriety possible.

Fear that does not constitute an obsession can be corrected by the philosophy provided in our AA program. Fear is nothing more or less than a distorted faith in the negative things of life and the evils *that might beset us.*

AA philosophy does not concern itself with anxiety or fear. As alcoholics, we were once unstable because of problems and anxieties that seemed impossible to remedy. The spiritual concepts of this program have removed them and have replaced them with peace of mind. We no longer worry; we have received a spiritual reprieve. This reprieve is extended from day to day by God in recognition of our appreciation of His help and the unselfish service we render to others.

Our antidote for fear is faith, not the distorted faith in fear, but rehabilitating all-out faith in God as we understand Him. We have found this to be an effective measure in overcoming all fears the alcoholic is subjected to.

ANGER

Anger in itself is a legitimate feeling, but it can be misused by indulging in it or by dumping it unfairly on others. An alcoholic whose emotions are dominated by anger, either overt or covert and unexpressed, will not progress in the program until he or she has dealt with the destructive effects of such anger.

Often the alcoholic combines anger and self-pity and feels victimized by the world; the alcoholic can then justify abusive behavior on the ground that others deserved it or "asked for it." This type of destructive anger is identified in the Big Book as a dangerous emotion for alcoholics: "If we were to live, we had to be free from anger. The grouch and the brainstorm were not for us. They may be the dubious luxury of normal men, but for alcoholics these things are poison."* Here, the Big Book speaks of the corrosive anger that is either held onto and never expressed, or the explosive outbursts of abusive anger that is common to many alcoholics. These feelings can lead back to self-pity and resentment, and cause slips.

In everyday life, alcoholics will meet situations that

---

*Read page 66, Chapter Five, in *Alcoholics Anonymous*.

will provoke anger. Alcoholics are not saints, and we are not perfect; we will still feel and experience anger. The important thing is to check yourself from venting anger unjustly upon someone else, or from holding onto anger and letting it turn into a resentment, or from turning it inward upon yourself so you feel unworthy and depressed. Anger can be cleanly expressed in a non-threatening and nonabusive way, and then you can let go. Usually the alcoholic will find some other, deeper emotion behind the anger, such as fear or sadness. Anger is often a cover-up for our feelings of inadequacy.

The alcoholic is only human. Alcoholics are subject to all human impulses and are often faced with conditions that arouse anger, but we need not be ignorant of the potential destructiveness of unexamined anger or the inroads its impulses can make upon recovery.

In compiling our inventories let us keep in mind the fact that we are alcoholics; that we are sick physically, mentally, and spiritually; that we have been unable to recover from our illness through our own efforts; and that thousands of alcoholics before us have effected their recovery by exchanging their alcoholic personalities for the happy, sober person-alities brought about by the AA way of living. With this is mind, we call upon a *Power greater than ourselves* to help guide us in making a searching and fearless moral inventory of ourselves as one of the Steps necessary for recovery from our illness, alcoholism.

BLIND SPOTS

Despite our sincere efforts to make honest inventories of all "the flaws in our makeup that caused our failure," some defects will not be recorded. Why? Simply because we fail to see them. Our mental and moral vision has been blinded too long by alcoholic reservation and rationalization. It is necessary to reserve space in our inventories for the blind spots we will later uncover. We should not worry about these undisclosed defects but tolerate their existence and let AA as a way of life reveal them. We then list them for correction.

SUMMARIZATION. Having decided to let God direct our will and unmanageable lives, we step out of the driver's seat to inspect our alcoholic personalities. We make "a searching and fearless moral inventory of ourselves," *not as psychiatrists but as sick lay people* who need simple understanding of our ills and defects—things that God will sublimate or help us outgrow. AA personality changes begin from such honest evaluation.

Pages 64-71 in Chapter Five of the Big Book suggest innumerable character defects, common to alcoholics, that should be listed in a written inventory. From our inventories we learn the spiritual illness of resentment and dishonesty; the frustration of jealousy, suspicion, self-pity, fear, anger, and false pride; and the harmful nature of criticism, intolerance, and vindictiveness.

We vitalize our deadened conscience as we catalog our devastating, self-centered habits. We learn to discern between right and wrong as we make our inventories honest, written records. This written inventory may be the difference between sobriety and another drunk.

Step Five

*Admitted to God, to ourselves, and to
another human being the exact nature
of our wrongs.*

If we have been honest and thorough with our personal inventories, we have listed and analyzed our character defects and have a record of the harm we have caused others.

We have a list of our greater handicaps, imperfections and the names of the people who have suffered as a result of our unmanageable lives and insane behavior.

These facts indicate certain defects in our lives; they constitute the record we have made of our wrongs. We have ascertained our defects and not only propose to correct them, but also to prepare a plan of action that will bring restitution and happiness to the men and women who have suffered mental, physical, or financial harm as a direct result of our uncontrolled drinking.

Step Five is a preparatory Step to the restitution that we expect to make as we carry out the provisions of Step Nine, where amends are necessary and we make them.

The exact nature of our wrongs is now admitted to God and ourselves and then talked over with a *third person.*

Alcoholic rationalization balks at this honest procedure, discounting the need of admitting anything to *another human being.*

The founders of our movement knew the value of doing this; they knew that only by so doing could we acquire the humility, honesty, and spiritual help necessary to live the AA program successfully.

Most of us saw our self-appraisals as exact; because we had conceded to God the error or our former alcoholic thought and conduct, we saw no need to go further. We reasoned God knew and would forgive us, so the matter was closed.

This is sugarcoated alcoholic thinking. It follows the old pattern and is but a pretense, a new form of escape from responsibility. We must give our long-hoarded secrets to another person if we are to gain peace of mind, self-respect, and recovery from alcoholism.

The humility this Step brings us is necessary to our future welfare. We will have no spiritual inspiration, no release from anxiety and fear, until we remove the skeletons from our closet. We must stop dodging people and start facing facts and issues if freedom from dread and tension is to be ours.

Step Five is a pivotal step. It calls for action that starts a real spiritual awakening as we back up our *faith with verbal works.*

If this Step seems difficult to you (and it may well seem that way), remember you are no exception. Many of us experienced the same reaction. This reaction is nothing more than the reflexes of a dying alcoholic personality trying to avoid reality: too little time has elapsed between our sudden change from an alcoholic's rationalization to that of rehabilitative conduct necessary to our program. We are unconsciously dominated by our old thoughts. These are but momentary thoughts of rebellion. They will quickly give way to the sublimating power of our new philosophy if we will be open-minded and have faith that God will aid us in arriving at the right solution.

The Step specifically outlines the action to be taken. When the right time arrives, arrange an interview with anyone outside of AA who will be *understanding but unaffected* by your narration.* We should not take this Step with anyone who might not respect our confidences. For this reason, a clergy member, psychiatrist, counselor, or doctor is our best bet. Most of these people are qualified to hear our stories, but clergy members are preferred because they have dedicated their lives to the service of God and fellow human beings.

There is no stated time for taking this Step—it is not to be rushed into. We do not take it as a form that must be complied with. There is a state of mind that will arise in all sincere members who are living the AA philosophy which will indicate clearly when they are ready. When this time arrives, however, we must act at once. To postpone taking it is inconsistent with our plan of recovery.

If in doubt about when to take Step Five—take it immediately. It is far better to take it before we think we are ready than to postpone it and not take it at all. Many members with years of sobriety in AA find that taking Step Five from time to time helps them to maintain their contented sobriety. Step Five brings mental and spiritual catharsis and perhaps should be taken periodically.

*Read paragraphs six and seven, Chapter Six, in *Alcoholics Anonymous*.

You are now engaged in a business deal with God and another human being. If our inventory has been thorough, we are in a position to "pocket our pride," to tell a story that will illuminate "every twist of character, every dark cranny of the past."* You have no reason to doubt the psychological and spiritual value offered. You will be well rewarded for your effort and will find yourself at a loss to express in words the gratification that will be yours. *Understanding of such things comes only with experience.*

Interpretation of the deep significance of admitting our wrongs to God, ourselves, and another human being is logically summed up by saying, "Once we have taken this step, withholding nothing, we are delighted. We can look the world in the eye. . . . We begin to feel the nearness of our Creator. We may have had certain spiritual beliefs, but now we begin to have a spiritual experience."**

SUMMARIZATION. The metamorphosis from the alcoholic to the new AA personality becomes more evident upon completion of Step Five. We are impressed with the simplicity of this effective spiritual device that started our spiritual awakening. The Step is a direct challenge to our sincerity, because we have

---

*Read Page 75, Chapter Six, of *Alcoholics Anonymous.*
**Read page 75, Chapter Six, in *Alcoholics Anonymous.*

been promised humility, a spiritual experience, and loss of fear when we have talked over our defects with a third person.

This is the one Step in the program that advises us what to do when we have completed it. This advice is given in our Big Book. It says, "Returning home we find a place where we can be quiet for an hour, carefully reviewing what we have done. We thank God from the bottom of our heart that we know Him better. Taking this book down from our shelf we turn to the page which contains the twelve steps. Carefully reading the first five proposals we ask if we have omitted anything, for we are building an arch through which we will walk a free man at last. Is our work solid so far? Are the stones properly in place? Have we skimped on the cement put into the foundation? Have we tried to make mortar without sand?

"If we can answer to our satisfaction, we then look at *Step Six*."*

---

*Read page 75 to the top of page 76, Chapter Six, in *Alcoholics Anonymous*.

STEPS SIX AND SEVEN

*Were entirely ready to have God remove
all these defects of character.*

*Humbly asked Him to remove
our shortcomings.*

It is only after we have completed Step Five, when humility has been experienced and self-respect has been restored as a result of our admitting to God and to another human being the exact nature of our wrongs, that we are in a suitable spiritual condition to carry out the provisions of Steps Six and Seven sincerely.

This action brings a new feeling of moral strength. For the first time we are facing our *real selves*—the selves whose withered roots have touched and are now drawing up an unfailing source of assurance, power, and security.

We find in the consummation of these Steps a *new peace*, a release from *tension* and *anxiety* as we now are laying our misconceptions and defects of character in

God's hands. We are asking Him to rid them from our lives. We are exerting great mental cooperation with God. We feel an intense humility that cries out for recognition and divine help.

The *Spiritual Lift*, the nearness to our Creator that is experienced from humble invocation of His help, and our willingness to be freed from old willful thoughts and habits are essential to successful attainment of these Steps.

The mental hygiene and spiritual house-cleaning we have started in our inventories and continued in Step Five reach their climax in Step Seven when we fully subject our wills to God and wish to surrender to Him all our moral imperfections.

The several objectives of Steps Six and Seven are:

1. To become honest and humble. To willingly seek God's help without reservation.
2. To perfect ourselves in the practice of unselfish prayer.
3. To be aware of our defective character traits.
4. To desire their removal.
5. To surrender completely all defects of character.
6. To believe God *can* remove them.
7. To ask Him to take them *all away.*

The results we expect from pursuit of these objectives are:

1. A reconciliation to God's way of doing business. We become "fed up" with our way and with further practice of trying to run the show ourselves.
2. A willingness to work out a plan for suppression of self-centeredness through faith and a conscious contact with God.
3. To experience dissatisfaction as a result of our alcoholic practices and to seek a spiritual inspiration that will bring us an inner sense of peace and security.
4. Increased faith, clean hearts and minds, ability to offer unselfish prayer.
5. A spiritual courage that is fearless in its outlook on life; a desire to make restitution to those our drinking has harmed.
6. A desire to quit bluffing and honestly give God a chance to remove from our lives all that stands in the way of our usefulness to Him and to others. True humility.
7. Elimination of our defective character traits, acquisition of peace of mind, and sobriety.

The spiritual attitude and satisfactory frame of mind necessary to effective fulfillment of these Steps have been progressively worked toward in the completion of the first five Steps of our program.

Knowledge of our illness, alcoholism, prompts us to turn to God for help. The alcoholic must pray. There is no standard form of prayer to use. Our remorse over past mistakes and a genuine desire to correct them will indicate how we shall pray.

We all come before God as sick people. We offer no alibis. We have no defense. We stand before Him subject to the weakness of alcoholism. We ask for an understanding of this illness and for His strength and help in arresting it. We wish to arrest it, but only for unselfish purposes. We ask forgiveness for the wrongs we have committed. We ask for protection from self-pity, from resentment, from all selfishness. We ask for wisdom and understanding to know His will. We ask for spiritual and physical strength to execute His will. Acknowledging our shortcomings, we sincerely pray to God that He will remove them.

Prayer, our highest type of mental energy, serves a threefold purpose. By it we ask God's help; we thank Him for recovery; and we maintain our contented sobriety.

There is nothing outstanding about an alcoholic's prayer to God. It is just a simple, sincere affair. The alcoholic has nothing to lose but stands to gain sobriety, sane behavior, peace of mind, and happiness for him- or herself and his or her family.

There is latent power within each of us that develops through conscious contact with God. It replaces alcoholic fear and weakness with spiritual strength and understanding. Through it the miracle of AA is possible.

Steps Six and Seven utilize this contact which thousands of alcoholics have humbly used in removing their defects of character.

These two Steps contain the forge that heats and forms the separate links that go into the new personality chains we are building. *Without them our rehabilitation is impossible.*

SUMMARIZATION. Restoration of our mental and spiritual health is in direct proportion to our recognized need for help and our willingness to work for recovery. Dishonesty, brain damage, indifference, and reservations are the only limitations to our recovery.

Reservations are those attitudes that oppose selfevaluation, cooperation, honesty, tolerance, forgiveness, faith, love, and unselfish prayer. These character defects stand between us and contented sobriety. They perpetuate spiritual illness. Recovery from alcoholism is dependent upon their removal.

A divine type of surgery is suggested by Steps Six and Seven. Humble prayer becomes the spiritual scalpel with which God cuts the damaged portions from our sick personalities. Complete surrender to God's will assures us a painless, successful operation.

Surrender of our defects to a Higher Power is not the spiritless act of a defeatist; it is the intelligent act of an alcoholic who replaces fear and weakness with spiritual courage, understanding, strength, and contented sobriety. So we "humbly ask[ed] Him to remove our shortcomings."

STEPS EIGHT AND NINE

*Made a list of all persons we had harmed,
and became willing to make amends
to them all.*

*Made direct amends to such people
wherever possible, except when to do so
would injure them or others.*[*]

The objective of Steps Eight and Nine is to *outline* and put into *practice* a working course of conduct which will directly rectify the harm or injury our drinking may have imposed upon others. We can then start relating harmoniously to God and to other people.

The practice of the Alcoholics Anonymous philosophy adequately fulfills these requirements. It is a proven *way of life* by which the alcoholic corrects past mistakes and makes restitution to relatives, friends, or enemies. This is done while the alcoholic

---

[*]Read paragraphs fourteen and fifteen, Chapter Six, of *Alcoholics Anonymous.*

effects his or her recovery from the physical, mental, and spiritual ravages of alcoholism.

Many alcoholics agree to the effectiveness of our philosophy but fail to benefit from it because they have not properly evaluated their alcoholic illness. Not believing themselves to be sick, they see no reason for inconveniencing themselves to get well. Reservations about their spiritual illness create indifference to the making of amends.

Members do not arrest alcoholism or gain recovery by merely agreeing with the principles of AA philosophy—*they recover only if they live them.*

These Steps work in conjunction with each other. We have a list of those we have harmed, we have our grudge list, and we have a list of those we are financially obligated to. Few of us realize that our own names head the list of those we have wronged and that by living this program we are first making amends to ourselves, to our outraged bodies, to our confused minds, and to our troubled spirits.

It is not difficult to list the people who suffered because we drank. Our real problem is to arrive at a state of mind that concedes the damage we have done and embraces a sincere willingness to amend it.

Step Nine is not easily or quickly carried out. Some restitution is started upon our acceptance of the AA program as a way of life. This is usually quite limited as it is not until we have spent several months in AA and have fortified our sobriety with good fundamental knowledge of the program that we acquire the spiritual courage and understanding to make discreet reparations.

The member is confronted with many obstacles in observance of this Step. We find procrastination a hindrance to some members. This should be avoided. On the other hand, there are those who are too ambitious to rebuild; they try to get the process over with at once. Remember, in most cases you will require a lifetime to complete Step Nine. Some members, under inspiration of the new personalities they are creating, become emotional and act on the spur of the moment. Their hasty action is apt to fall short of accomplishment. Pride is another barrier. Confusion, through improper interpretation of the purpose of Step Nine, is a common handicap.

The older members will be helpful, if consulted, wherever perplexities are encountered. Do not act hastily or in doubt. Invite their opinions. Then formulate a plan of action and with God's help start correcting your wrongs.

Meditation and prayer are necessary to make amends. No amend should be made that is not preceded by prayer as it will lack complete purpose and effectiveness. Conscious contact with God in making amends will not only bring about a more satisfactory result, but it will aid you in avoiding amends that might injure others. Discretion in this connection is imperative.*

God's presence in our lives now alters and sublimates our mental and physical activities. It gives us the humility we need to make amends and an incentive to get started. *We are trying to put our lives in order. We do this through maximum service to God and the people about us.*

The questions now arise: Whose names belong on our list? How do we go about making amends to these people? What procedure do we follow?

Our answers to these questions are found in *Alcoholics Anonymous* in Chapter Six, under discussion on Steps Eight and Nine.

The following summary of certain advice taken from those pages is incomplete and must be enlarged upon by each member in application to his or her particular needs.

We find it impossible to cover this complex matter in its entirety, but we have listed a few suggestions

---

*Read pages 76-84, Chapter Six, of *Alcoholics Anonymous*.

and examples for guidance. Our list classifies four types of people to make amends to. The list comments on the fifth type of people who are not generally included in the list, yet these people must constantly be considered if daily sobriety is to be assured.

GROUP ONE: FRIENDS

This group includes people who have been close friends; business associates; those who we should be friendly toward, but we have severed connections with them because of resentments, pride, or fancied wrongs; those we have treated unjustly but have not been harmed aside from harsh words or acts of asinine behavior; and those who we are not financially indebted to.

We should approach these people with sincerity. Our approach is calm, frank, and open. We aim to convince such people of our good intentions and to assure them that we regret how we treated them.

We explain our alcoholic illness, the nature of resentments and hatred in relation to our sobriety. We outline our good intentions and ask forgiveness and cooperation in our future associations. Our purpose is to create good will and regain friendship.

We avoid impressing anyone with the idea that we

are religious fanatics, but we never sidestep the spiritual issue or deny God if He is brought into the conversation.

We do not attempt amends to those who are still smarting from a recent injustice and never make any amends that will harm another person.

There will be few cases where our advances will be rejected. If we are unable to establish a reconciliation and are not favorably received, we simply drop the matter in hopes that eventually our sobriety and future dealings will repair the breach between us.

The main points to keep in mind are we are out to perform a duty, we will not be upset or discouraged by gruff or unpleasant receptions, the intent of our visit is a harmonious one, and *under no circumstances will we live in an angry or resentful mood.*

GROUP TWO: FAMILIES*

The people under this group are generally found in our families. The outstanding examples are the spouses of alcoholics. The people who follow are the mothers, fathers, sons, daughters, and often close friends whose lives we have "kept in turmoil because of our selfish and inconsiderate habits." We have been

---

*Read Chapter Nine, "The Family Afterward," in *Alcoholics Anonymous.*

"like a tornado roaring our way through the lives of others," breaking hearts and killing "sweet relationships." The damage we have done to this group has been spread over many years. It will take many years to amend it.

The manner of our approach should be no problem unless homes have been broken up and separation makes reparation impossible. Even then we will benefit from living the program, as our record of sobriety usually comes to the attention of the injured one. Time may be required to effect reconciliation, but satisfactory adjustments are generally forthcoming. Often this has been handled through correspondence, but direct contact is preferable in all cases wherever possible.

If the home is still intact, family members are aware of the alcoholic's desire to treat the alcoholic illness, and they seldom fail to back the alcoholic in this purpose.

It is important that they read *Alcoholics Anonymous*, to gain an understanding of alcoholism and the Steps outlined in our program for its treatment. A new member needs the full understanding and cooperation of the family. The alcoholic's amends to them are more thorough and are made with greater ease when the family realizes what the alcoholic is trying to do.

Our sobriety is a blessing to the individuals in Group Two. As a rule, it is the greatest single amend we can make to them, yet it is a partial amend that must be followed with kind and thoughtful acts.* Sobriety in itself is not enough. We must be attentive and considerate of the family as a whole. Harmony and cooperation should be established. Evidence of our love and a desire to become worthy of their respect will be most helpful. Irreparable damage is not unusual. When encountered it can only be offset by obvious manifestation of our willingness to correct the condition, if possible. We lose no time in making the amends that are possible.

Sex-related problems complicate the lives of many alcoholics. The first consideration in handling them is to stop the trouble at its source. Honesty is a prime factor in the lives of all members and leaves no room for adultery.

Injury to others must be considered in straightening out sex-related problems. We always use great tact in handling the situation if amends are in order. Jealousy, when aroused, greatly impedes our

---

*Read Chapter Eight, "To Wives," in *Alcoholics Anonymous*.

progress. Fairness, meditation, and prayer must be relied upon. We lay the matter in God's hands and are then guided by the dictates of His will and our conscience.

GROUP THREE: CREDITORS

"We do not dodge our creditors."* The creditor usually knows about our drinking. If not, we should lay our cards on the table. If payment is impossible, we arrange the best deal we can. Repayment may begin on a future date, or we may begin making small payments, increasing these amounts when we are financially stronger. The main idea is *to have an understanding.* We must be at ease in this connection, otherwise fear may return us to drinking. When creditors understand the nature of our alcoholic illness they will readily see money cannot be repaid unless we maintain sobriety; they will then be in a better mood to receive our proposition.

GROUP FOUR: THE DECEASED

The harm we have done to departed relatives or friends is often cause for self-condemnation. This should not be; it is a harmful practice. We treat self-

---

*Read the second paragraph on page 78, Chapter Six, in *Alcoholics Anonymous.*

condemnation with intelligent prayer.

We must realize the futility of remorse over wrongs that we cannot amend. We do not allow such errors of the past to impair our future usefulness. We reason that the harm done will be partially offset by the new philosophy we are living; even though we cannot reach the departed one we can still make amends to living relatives. If this is impossible we resort to God in prayer, asking Him to see the willingness in our hearts and to forgive us in connection with these people.

Then there are *the amends we must daily make to God.* These become automatic; they are the requirements of each of the Twelve Steps. The AA program is *one big amend* broken into twelve parts.

Before we can settle the harm done to others we must eliminate the source of moral and physical devastation within ourselves.

Alcoholism is our illness. It caused the injuries we imposed on our families, friends, and those loved ones who have departed. It accounts for our indebtedness; it is responsible for our impaired physical condition; it has brought us irrational thinking, insane behavior, and spiritual illness.

We make amends to ourselves—to the personalities we were before becoming alcoholic—by understanding our sickness, by illuminating our defects of character, by eliminating them from our lives, by intelligent physical care of our bodies, by restoration of our mental apparatus through sobriety, and by treatment of our spiritual illness through recourse to understanding and practicing God's Will. The alcoholic's rehabilitation is contingent upon amends and will be *as long as he or she lives.*

We are often inclined to clutter our list with petty wrongs long forgotten and of no importance. Amends of this sort would never end; they should be forgotten. Many of us have been uncertain over the advisability of making some amends. The yardstick to use in this connection is your conscience; if the wrong bothers you it should undoubtedly be amended.

The people covered in this discussion will not comprise a full list of those to whom we make amends. There will be others on our list and we will find that new errors constantly occurring in our lives will send us back to make reparation to those already on the list.

Step Nine has reclaimed many broken friendships; it has brought peace and happiness to the lives of those who suffered because of our alcoholism. Its great rehabilitative power has also affected the lives of thousands of alcoholics through the spiritual awakening they have experienced. Because of this Step, these same alcoholics have recovered their self-respect, they have taken on courage and confidence, and they have assumed responsibility. They sense God's presence, and with His presence comes the realization that their lives are again becoming manageable.

SUMMARIZATION. We can hardly overestimate the importance of making amends. Most of us underestimate its power to change our attitude toward God, our fellow human beings, and everyday circumstances of sober living.

Our bid for a new lease on life, for the tolerance and forgiveness we expect from others, should prompt us to respond with tolerance, forgiveness, and amends. AA teaches us that to "live and let live" is to safeguard our sobriety.

Resentful attitudes toward others will defeat our recovery. We correct this attitude in the practice of Step Nine. Amends integrate our personalities by harmonious, helpful relations with God and the victims of our insane, alcoholic obsession. We cannot hate and make amends at the same time.

Admitting and rectifying wrongs is a regenerative process necessary to our rehabilitation. It brings us spiritual understanding and develops spiritual strength that contribute to contented sobriety.

The Twelve Steps are one big amend that we make to God and to ourselves. Self-preservation demands this. We pay our creditors. We come clean with God and make amends to loyal friends and relatives except when to do so might be harmful to them or others.

Attitudes of reservation and unwillingness are dangerous for us. They fill us with discontent and belligerency that result in drunkenness.

We are trying to put our lives in order. We do this through maximum service to God and the people about us. We believe this is the purpose of Steps Eight and Nine.

STEP TEN

*Continued to take personal inventory
and when we were wrong
promptly admitted it.* [*]

Step Ten is one of the maintenance Steps. Its purpose is to remind us that moral defects—selfishness, dishonesty, resentment, and fear—are still problems we will encounter daily. These defects remain serious threats to our sobriety. AA suggests a daily inventory to disclose our harmful thoughts and actions. Admitting mistakes is indispensable to our inventory and sobriety.

George A. Dorsey contributes a bit of interesting information on the instability of human nature by saying, "Man is something happening all the time; he is a going concern, he makes his rules, revises his formulae and recasts his mould in the act of being and while going. *It is in man's nature that he does not stay put.*"

---

[*] Read pages 84-85, Chapter Six, in *Alcoholics Anonymous.*

This Step provides a daily self-inventory to check our mental and spiritual status.

Through it we avoid the unhappy experiences that result when we are dominated by forms of self-centeredness that creep back into our lives.

We make the inventory a sort of intelligence department that identifies old and new moral defects. It has a rogues' gallery where we catalog each defect and its alias. So when self-centeredness, for instance, disguises itself as complacency or boredom, we detect the deception, then arrest and treat it.

These defects are great sources of danger to us. They had much to do with the injuries once suffered from abnormal drinking. They can still return us to the insanity of alcoholism.

Step Four provided us with an inventory that served a definite purpose. It exposed character defects we formerly refused to recognize—defects that made our lives unmanageable. The necessity for listing and removing these personality flaws becomes increasingly obvious as we add new days to our record of sober living.

The inventory supplied us with an understanding of our problem. It brought us face-to-face with ourselves, with our shortcomings—with the sense of removing them through God's help. It was indispensable at the time but fulfilled its intended use once the nature of our self-willed alcoholic habits and defects were recorded. Without this record, progress in AA would have been impossible.

Because of this record, progress has been made. Knowledge of our moral defects and practice of the AA program have completely changed our lives. It has improved our attitudes toward God, our daily problems, and our feelings toward fellow human beings.

We have gained the confidence and the respect of others. Many of our friends have expressed their admiration for the sobriety we have acquired; peace and satisfaction naturally follow this accomplishment. We enjoy our security and the friendly attitude of those about us.

Step Ten will safeguard this progress if we continue our personal inventories and promptly admit it when we are wrong.

We can't forget alcoholics never seem to stay put. Our founders knew this from their experiences. They knew drinking habits of long standing would cry to be repeated.

They knew new character defects will appear, and many old defects will reappear in disguised forms. Hence, we need daily mental checkups to announce the advent of old habits and act as sentries to detect new defects.

Avoid confusing the respective functions of Steps Four and Ten.

Step Four was a written inventory that listed our alcoholic character defects and the people we had harmed. We left it open for future additions.

Step Ten is the AA slide rule for quick mental reckoning of daily AA progress—a perpetual mental inventory that safeguards our waking hours of sobriety and an appraisal to close each day.

The plan of our philosophy is to *live each Step*. The object of Step Ten is to continue our personal inventory and daily check the progress we make with each Step in the AA program.

By reviewing them we often find ourselves "off the beam." This is a bad spot for an alcoholic who invariably goes whole hog if immediate steps toward correction are not taken.

Correction is possible if we realize our danger when our inventories reveal it to us. Prompt action upon such discovery is necessary. It is not unusual to find ourselves off the beam; the idea is to get back on again. The daily inventory is essential to this requirement.

Members may recognize a few of the off the beam positions in the following tendencies:

1. When we have forgotten we are alcoholics—we have nervous systems that are incapable of withstanding the narcotic effect of alcohol.
2. When complacency lowers our guard and allows resentment and intolerance to creep back into our lives.
3. When we ease up on the practice of honesty, humility, and making amends.
4. When we become cocky over our AA success and cease contact with God.
5. When we lack interest in new members and feel it inconvenient to help them.
6. When we demand authority or expect praise for our sobriety.
7. When boredom makes an appearance.
8. When we start missing AA meetings.
9. When we stop studying the AA Book.

When our inventories disclose any of these symptoms, we stand in jeopardy of drinking. Our serious problem is self-centeredness. Further investigation will unearth a severe case of spiritual congestion.

The antidote is a quick review of our alcoholism. We should pray for renewed interest. Read the Big Book. Talk AA with the members. Sincerely interest ourselves in our AA group. Attend more meetings. Do our bit. Consider our alcoholism as arrested but never cured. Lose ourselves in the program. Work with new members. Review the miracle that God has performed in our lives. Be honest and thankfully offer a prayer of gratitude. Always carry the AA book on out of town trips.

The second part of Step Ten, "...when we were wrong promptly admitted it," is not to be taken lightly. It is a good character conditioner. Recognition of a wrong is not enough; verbal acknowledgment should follow. The requirement of our program is to make amends if the wrong has harmed anyone. The inventory keeps us alert to our responsibility in this matter.

Sincere members will apply these things to themselves. They will search out the significance of admitting it when we are wrong.

Let us remember, in Step Five we admitted to God, to ourselves, and to another human being the exact nature of our wrongs. We meditated on our shortcomings in Steps Six and Seven. It was vital to our well-being at the time.

It is still vital. We haven't changed in that respect and we never will. Alcoholism has been arrested, but it has not been cured.

It is not in the nature of the alcoholic to stay put. We must admit our wrongs to receive the feelings of decency and worthiness that keep us in the right mental and spiritual condition to maintain contented, permanent sobriety.

Continue this inventory daily. When we are wrong, we can understand the value of getting it off our chests at once. Admit our mistakes. It is stupid to defend our blunders. Get rid of that habit.* Remember, *our new personality is not compatible with moral defects or concealed errors.*

Step Ten makes us self-critical and less apt to criticize others. It keeps us on the beam.

We do not make a farce of our lives when we employ our inventories. We should check ourselves thoroughly to make real headway. We owe it to God, ourselves, and our families. We must think sober to live sober.

The inventory will help us determine the degree of success we are attaining in AA. It will let us know

---

*Observance and practice of this Step will give us knowledge and develop our capacity to use it. Step Ten will create a stable mental balance that helps provide the spiritual condition so necessary in our recovery from alcoholism.

where we stand. It will keep us in *good standing*.

SUMMARIZATION. Nothing is more important to the recovering alcoholic than the maintenance of contented sobriety.

Step Ten affords such maintenance. It is a simple, effective means of sounding the hazardous shoals of mental drunkenness, for reservations, thoughts, moods, or acts might return us to physical drunkenness. Self-centeredness remains a dire threat.

We safeguard our daily sobriety by frequent mental audits of our behavior and willingness to admit mistakes. We make the personal inventory a daily habit. It will uncover many negative thoughts and willful behaviors that need correction by the dictates of our conscience. By closing the day with a review of our emotional conduct and our treatment of others, we can discover and correct both our willfulness and mistakes.

Admitting our mistakes brings both psychological and spiritual benefits. They complement the personal inventory. They quicken our conscience, alerting us to knowledge of our need for God's help, for divine sublimation of our will, and for continued practice of Step Ten.

STEP ELEVEN

Sought through prayer and meditation to improve our conscious contact with God as we understood Him, praying only for knowledge of His will for us and the power to carry that out.

This Step can be broken into three parts. Let us first consider that part which recommends the need for prayer and meditation to improve our understanding of God, our contact with Him.

A prayer for improved contact with God, for knowledge of His will, and for mental, physical, and spiritual energy to carry it out, requires the coordinated effort of all our faculties.

We know this Step is needed, because of the past experiences of AA members who forgot they have not been *cured* of alcoholism. They have mistaken recovery for cure, so after a few months of sobriety have considered practice of the AA philosophy unnecessary. They have overlooked the tendency to forget the pain and sorrow suffered from the disease. They take their changed personalities *too much for granted,* assuming that once acquired these personalities will always stay with them.

God's help was needed in their dire emergency, but that has since passed. They say, "We will never drink again; we never even think about it." They let down their guard and ease up on spiritual contacts and service.

A positive attitude toward permanent sobriety is commendable, but only recommended as it applies to each twenty-four-hour period.

The fact that we have no desire or intention to drink again is a favorable frame of mind for new members. It is our ambition, a mental condition to be grateful for, *but one that too often fosters complacency which can lead us into trouble unless God is given proper credit for the sobriety we enjoy.*

When complacency develops we are apt to forget the part that God has played in effecting our rehabilitation. We overlook the fact that our nervous systems are still those of alcoholics. We seem to forget that as alcoholics we are susceptible to moods and emotions that we formerly appeased with alcohol. Complacency obscures the knowledge that our recovery from alcoholism was granted by a *Power greater than ourselves.* Without contact with God, returning to former physical and spiritual lows is probable.

Cooperation with a *Power greater than ourselves* has pulled us out of the alcoholic rut. Step Eleven is a maintenance Step that was planned to keep us out of the rut and make us stay put.

It keeps us spiritually active and in tune with God. It insures against the dulling of inspiration as our alcoholic problems diminish.

Understanding of this situation and the knowledge that members do get "off the beam" spiritually at times is our first line of defense. We fortify this defense by keeping this uppermost in our minds: In reality we are on a "daily reprieve," and our reprieves are "contingent on the maintenance of our spiritual condition."*

The bitter experiences of members who insist upon learning the hard way—the backsliders who returned to drinking—attest to the truth of this statement.

Their trouble invariably *begins with neglect of prayer.* It slowly matures as they abandon conscious contact with God and service to others.

Our realizations of God's help in the past impresses us with the fact that it can be utilized even better in

---

*Read page 85, Chapter Six, of *Alcoholics Anonymous.*

the future. A sure way of increasing this help and improving our contact with God is through simple prayers of sincere gratitude. We can meditate on the help He has given, acknowledge its source, and be genuine in our thanks for His understanding of our alcoholic problem and the strength He has given us to overcome it.

He has demonstrated a miracle in our lives. We have been freed from alcohol and compulsive drinking. We have acquired sobriety and are enjoying its benefits. Through it we have regained health and mental stability and have built up self-respect within ourselves, at home, and among our friends. It is our privilege and duty to safeguard and protect this miracle. It was accomplished through humility, faith, and prayer as we actively tried to understand and carry out His will.

Prayers of gratitude are especially good for alcoholics. They kill egoism and awaken us to life's true values. Try contacting God with thanks and appreciation. He renews our faith with answers to such prayer. We need endless experience in the practice of unselfish prayer to balance the spiritual debits alcoholism has charged against us.

Each member will naturally have his or her technique for improving conscious contact with God, but if actual prayers of gratitude are missing, the technique should be enlarged to include them. It is more sensible to ask God for a changed circumstance after you have acknowledged and expressed thanks for your present circumstances.

Prayer and meditation to improve our conscious contact with God seem easiest when we are relaxed and composed (when strife, fear, and resentment are laid aside) and we are in harmony with those about us. For this reason it is advisable to consider the importance of mental composure and physical relaxation as far as prayer is concerned, and to comment upon them further as stabilizers to the restless nature of the alcoholic.

The Twelve Steps will lead many of us to recognize our need for spiritual help, but they do not directly point out that we may be abusing our source of physical and mental energy.

Relaxation of mind and body and surrender of our will to God are necessary before prayer and meditation are truly satisfying.

We owe God both humility and respect; we show it by freeing ourselves, for the moment, from material considerations, self-pity, fear, or anxiety, and by giving Him our undivided attention.

It is profitable for us to understand the value of keeping our bodies in a healthy condition, to practice poise and composure.

Alcoholics possess a restless spirit that tends toward overactivity. We not only practiced this by uncontrolled drinking, but we showed evidence of our intemperance in many other ways. Therefore we recommend relaxation as an aid to prayer and suggest that quiet time, aside from prayer, will be beneficial to all alcoholics.*

The habit of relaxation practiced during quiet times at intervals throughout each day is exactly what we need. Prominent medical authorities agree on this matter.

The intervals will be determined by our moods and mental attitudes, as well as our response to fear, anger, fatigue, emotional stress, and tension.

These feelings may be expressed by the alcoholic's behavior. They constitute a hazard that jeopardizes the chances of recovery.

These feelings were once relieved by drinking. We cannot ignore them now and expect to function normally or attain that degree of spiritual or mental efficiency which composure would bring us.

---

*Read the last four paragraphs of Chapter Six in *Alcoholics Anonymous*.

TREATMENT. We attempt to suspend all mental and physical activities momentarily. We try to relax our entire bodies, then close our minds to the worries and anxieties about us.

What do we think about? Just relaxation. Then we let go of our cares and turn to God with this simple prayer: *Thy Will Be Done.*

How long do we continue this? We can be our own judges. It can be a matter of minutes if necessary. We know, however, from experience, that even *thirty seconds of complete relaxation* of mind and body will do the trick. It is simple. Try it.

We owe it to ourselves and to the people about us. Our conscious contact with God is hardly complete without it.

The second part of this Step deals with *prayer for a knowledge of His will.* This knowledge will bring the proper use of our will, which seems to be tied up in self-denial and willing service to others.

The questions that have repeatedly confronted members are: What is God's will? How am I to know it from my own will?

In AA God's will for the alcoholic is sobriety. Other aspects embrace conscious contact with Him, faith, prayer, honesty, and humility. But, day by day, sobriety is the first essential of His will for us.

Members should quickly realize AA philosophy is not a religion. AA is a practical therapy for arresting the disease of alcoholism. The practice of the Twelve Steps in no way conflicts with any religion. It does not ask for divided loyalties any more than medical therapy in treatment of disease.

The will of God would be easier understood and executed if there were no one in the world to consider but ourselves.

We would not lie to ourselves as we do under the present circumstances; cheating would not only be unnecessary, it would be impossible. We could not commit adultery and there would be no excuse or occasion for leading a double life.

Drunkenness under such circumstances would not harm anyone but ourselves. Moral values would be entirely changed, making sin impossible unless we denied God completely. The nature of our prayer would have little resemblance to the prayer we now offer. The chief need we would have for God then would be that of personal contact to offset loneliness, to avert danger, to cure sickness, and to establish security in the world hereafter.

Such self-centered living would soon become boring beyond belief. We would long for human companionship, someone to share our lives with, to hear our tales of woe, and to minister to. Our successes and failures would mean little unless we could share them. Human happiness stems from faith in God, from human association, and from a desire to live and let live. That is the way God made us, and we cannot fulfill our destiny otherwise. Fortunately, we are not alone in this universe but are one of millions that are entirely dependent upon each other for the necessities of life and the peace of mind that makes living worthwhile.

Therefore, we deduce that our understanding of God's will *starts with surrender of our wills to Him and with charitable, loving acts of service to others. We cannot live unto ourselves alone.*

Our spiritual awakening is contingent upon our personality change. It results from renouncing self-will, from admitting our wrongs, from charitable deeds that benefit others at the expense of our own time and money, and from making amends. It was only while engaged in thought and activity of this nature that we keenly felt the presence of God, or came close to the knowledge of His will. The answer to our prayer for such understanding comes with the least effort when we are on spiritual missions of help and service, when our conscience guides us, and when we forgive and feel gratitude. Our efforts in this direction, aided by faith and prayer for guidance, will bring us near to God.

Daily practice of the Alcoholics Anonymous program keeps us close to the spiritual and physical needs of humanity. There is much work to be done in its rehabilitation. As we interest ourselves in this work and carry it on, *we are, to the best of our ability, gaining a knowledge of God's will by the practice of faith, honesty, and unselfish service.*

As active members, we are trying to carry the will of God into our daily lives; in doing so, we may encounter criticism either at home or by fellow members of AA. We are not discouraged by such criticism, *as long as our motives are sincere and constructive.* If we are wrong, we admit it and seek further understanding from God. We keep trying. We continue to have faith in our work and prayer.

Sometimes criticism of someone's actions is in order; if so, it can be of a constructive nature and not the result of resentment or envy. Our purpose is to conform to the will of God, never to oppose it.

The third part of this Step relates to prayer for the power to *carry out God's will.* This prayer is for *mental efficiency,* for *spiritual strength,* and for *physical endurance.*

We must merit the power we seek by first improving our efficiency. Mental energy, spiritual strength, and physical endurance are not granted until we qualify for them. We may pray for them, and we should, but they cannot be earned by merely asking. They must be earned by honest endeavor.

The power is developed as we surrender self-centeredness, and by prayer and meditation. We "improve our conscious contact with God" when we forgive and help others.

We cannot live others' lives, but we can help them help themselves. Our interest will urge them to renewed effort. As we aid their progress we enrich our own resourcefulness. As we help them develop strength we are unconsciously devising ways and means for gaining new power and understanding ourselves.

It is not wise to pray for power selfishly or with resentment, envy, or self-pity in our hearts. God grants spiritual help freely to honest alcoholics who try to live the AA program. His help is limited only by reservations and half-hearted application. Members who faithfully live the Twelve Steps to the best of their ability should pray frequently. God will answer their unselfish prayer.

At times our thinking becomes self-centered. We try to force issues. We mistake our willfulness for Divine Will, and by sheer willpower we accomplish certain objectives. The true source of such power soon becomes evident. We find ourselves out of harmony with other members. We lose that warm feeling of accomplishment. We lack proper inspiration. We are unappreciated and misunderstood. We do things that give us no pleasure and are not useful to others. When this occurs we may be sure the power we are generating has no connection with the *Power greater than ourselves.*

It is safe to use this comparison as a yardstick to gauge the source and quality of our power.

When we get no inspiration or happiness from our efforts we certainly are not in harmony with God or those about us. We should apply Step Ten at once. Admitting our mistakes and praying for spiritual aid will be most helpful. Follow up with outright service to someone else. God releases power to those whose lives are channels for His will. This takes us out of the "driver's seat" and back to the AA program.

We all suffer from spiritual apathy and misuse of our emotional energy. Perhaps we should restore spiritual balance by retaking Step Five.

Paradoxically, alcoholic emotions may either make

or break us. It seems necessary that we learn their constructive use.

There is a practical solution to our emotional problems, a procedure that responds to the intelligent application of facts that science has provided.

Experience teaches us which part our emotional behavior has played in acquiring and maintaining our alcoholic condition. Feelings of hate, criticism, resentment, self-pity, jealousy, and intolerance prolonged and aggravated the insane behavior of our compulsive drinking.

Psychology teaches us that *emotions and feelings are sources of energy.* Examples of this energy are found in fear, anger, sexual attraction, and love. Humans must have this emotional energy to function mentally and physically; without it we would be abnormal.

Without the drive of emotional energy we would be helpless, bedridden creatures. We would lack the capacity to engage in the daily routine of living. We would not think or move about. We would be practically immobile. We would retain our reflexes and little else.

As alcoholics, we have overlooked the value of harnessing the right emotional energy. We have used the energy of destructive, negative power at the expense of creative, positive power.

Obviously, we have instinctively used the drive from fear, sexual attraction, and anger. We have submitted our wills to these emotions, to the detriment of our spiritual well-being. We didn't realize we are unable to withstand the demands of such devastating energy.

We have overlooked a greater source of energy that we are capable of generating, that of love.

Human energy reaches its maximum and is most constructive when the mind and body are activated by this positive emotion.

It is reasonable to believe, therefore, that the *power to carry out God's will must come from the inspiration and energy that are found in the emotion, love—love that embraces God and humankind. We serve and appreciate both.*

SUMMARIZATION. We set up a definite twenty-four-hour discipline of our emotional conduct. We start each day with a morning quiet time praying for freedom from self-centeredness, fear, and dishonesty. Planning our day, we ask for knowledge of God's will and for divine direction that we may make right decisions. Our prayers should be unselfish and useful to others.

This Step recommends we relax and cease foolish waste of energy. We can establish a daily period for reading the Big Book, reading spiritual literature, clearing our minds of wrong motives, and learning to live and let live.

Each night we inventory our activities of that day. We admit the wrong we have done. We ask God's forgiveness and consult Him regarding amends to be made, closing our day with a prayer of appreciation for His help and our sobriety.[*]

---

[*]This summary is from the discussion of Step Eleven in *Alcoholics Anonymous*. See Chapter Six, pages 85-88. Study them and then set up your twenty-four-hour schedule of AA living.

STEP TWELVE

*Having had a spiritual awakening as the
result of these steps, we tried to carry this
message to alcoholics, and to practice these
principles in all our affairs.* *

The aim of this interpretation is to give the working
mechanics of Step Twelve. All references are from a
reliable source of information—*Alcoholics Anonymous.*

We can arrive at an understanding and practice of
this Step by studying each of its three divisions.

FIRST DIVISION

*"Having had a spiritual awakening as the result of these
steps . . ."*

Since this is an interpretation of established AA
concepts, it would be inconsistent to mince words over
spiritual values or to withhold the fact that a spiritual

---
*Read Step Twelve on page 60, Chapter Five, "How It Works," in
Alcoholics Anonymous.

awakening is an essential part of our recovery.

Providentially for us, at least, six of the Twelve Steps are of a spiritual nature. Knowing the fallacies of alcoholic thinking, it is inconceivable that we could recover from alcoholism without spiritual inspiration dependent upon some Power greater than our own. We get this inspiration and come to know God by living the Twelve Steps.

Without the spiritual principles of the Twelve Steps there could be no AA. Instead there would be a group of disgruntled alcoholics, temporarily on the wagon, living in a perpetual state of mental drunkenness.

Lacking the benefit of spiritual influence, the jungle law of resentful, alcoholic thinking would take over and drive each member back to the insanity of alcoholism. Our sobriety demands a personality change. We gain this in the form of a spiritual awakening from living the AA program.

Are we really spiritually awakened or is it chance, fear, self-will, or alcoholic rationalization that keeps us sober? If by the latter, then what fills us with the enthusiasm and the desire to carry the message to other alcoholics? Can this worthy motive result from chance, fear, or self-centeredness?

Who grants us the power to stop drinking and continue abstinence? Who grants us the power to help othe⁻ alcoholics stop drinking? Who grants us the desire to help them stop? What gives others the power to acquire and pass on the miracle of sobriety? Is it possible for alcoholics to arrest the physical allergy and the mental obsession of alcoholism by their own power? We think not. Medicine concurs. Alcoholics who try to disprove this theory end up drunk.

Obviously, there are but two answers to these questions. First: those who accept and try to live all of the Twelve Steps seldom fail in AA. Second: those who skip their spiritual principles seldom succeed.

Evidently, we require spiritual aid to attain the mental stability conducive to the sobriety we wish to enjoy.

A survey, in which several hundred AA members were interviewed, disclosed many interesting opinions concerning the relation of spiritual awakenings to their sobriety. Only members with one year or more of sobriety were contacted.

The following questions were casually put to each member.*

1. Did you have a spiritual awakening?
2. Was it vital to your recovery?

---

*Try these questions in a group meeting. They bring out excellent discussion.

3. When did it take place?
4. Can you define it?

Of those interviewed, most agreed they had undergone a profound personality change for the better. Only two persons laid claim to revolutionary spiritual transformations.

Both groups conceded the importance of a personality change to their sobriety and saw the evidence of a spiritual awakening in their willingness to accept God's help as they faced the problems of sober living.

Few members could recall when this had taken place. In many cases, close associates had noticed it first. Some were unable to define their conscious contact with God, yet each one claimed enough to stay sober.

Their experiences started with surrender of their character defects to God as they understood Him and grew as they relied upon Him instead of alcohol and self.

Opinions about spiritual awakenings, taken from members internationally, had common denominators of faith, surrender, humility, tolerance, and love. These elements cannot be listed in any order of importance. Each was important to the one who gave it.

Here are some of their convictions. "It is my honest belief that I was spiritually awakened when...

1. "...I realized that something had kept me away from that first drink. When my former skepticism about God left me and I took on more faith in AA—when I felt gratitude and humbly expressed it in prayer to 'God as I understood Him.'"

2. "...attending an AA meeting. I was greatly impressed by the talk of a six-month member who, obviously, wanted nothing short of contented sobriety. His willingness to come clean set me thinking. I had been sober for two years, but not happy about it. The next day, I took Step Five with an understanding clergyman. That was the start of my spiritual awakening."

3. "...my intelligence made me realize there must be a Power working within me, apart from my physical being, that had given me sobriety and peace of mind—both at the same time."

4. "...I first became aware of the good things I had that deserved gratitude and felt concern enough for the needs of others to try and help them—when, through dependence upon a Higher Power, I remained sober and regained confidence in myself again."

5. "...I willingly accepted my own understanding of God, not the ideas of someone else, but my own understanding."

6. "...I called AA for help and was treated with understanding, friendship, and compassion by my sponsors."

7. "...I fully admitted my helplessness as an alcoholic and knew that it would take Power outside of my own to save me from insanity or an alcoholic death. My awakening was progressive, to which each Step contributed its part."

8. "...at the end of my first month in AA, I was seized with a tremendous compulsion to drink. Halfway into a bar, I asked God for help. It came immediately. I left the place without a drink, with a prayer of gratitude in my heart."

9. "...after trying to live the spiritual principles of the Twelve Steps, I became convinced that I had done my first honest day's work and that I had really tried to make it a worthy day. It was then that I realized that I had not done it alone."

10. "...after my decision in Step Three, I started an inventory to find out what was separating me from the

God of my childhood. The awakening must have started when I discovered my conscience—when I listened to it and used it as a deciding factor in judging between right and wrong."

11. "...I could see the other person's viewpoint and make allowance for the other's shortcomings and admit my own, when I commenced to pray for that person's welfare, as well as my own."

12. "...I started making amends. The first one was favorably received and brought me a wonderful sense of satisfaction and well-being. I suspected this was of spiritual origin. But when I was nearly thrown out of a man's office and did not blow my top on the next call, I knew that God's will—not mine—was guiding me."

The findings of this survey did not indicate that time was the essence of a spiritual awakening, nor did the speed of the awakening have any bearing upon its depth or quality.

Some members acquired it quickly. Others required weeks and months of AA effort and association before they were awakened to an inner feeling of God's presence.

But regardless of the time or depth of these awakenings they all occurred to alcoholics as they sensed their character defects and tried to turn them over to God as they understood Him.

Were these experiences mere fantasies? Hardly! Sobriety and peace of mind came only with faith and dependence on God's will.

The newcomer is slow to recognize a spiritual awakening within the AA way of life. That is why our founders advised, "Both you and the new man must walk day by day in the path of spiritual progress."*

Few members sense the need or know the importance of AA's spiritual program in the daily upkeep of their sobriety. Lost in the confusing maze of their alcoholic dilemma, they think only in terms of escaping the physical and mental agony of their drinking. The quality of their sobriety does not seem important in the beginning.

Entering AA, it was hard to visualize a goal beyond wretched abstinence. Compulsive drinking had us in a bad spot. We could not live with alcohol, yet life seemed impossible without it. AA offered sobriety, but there were strings attached. It came in a spiritual package that some of us refused to accept.

---

*Read page 100, Chapter Seven, in *Alcoholics Anonymous*.

This was not surprising as we had been in conflict with God's will for many years. Talking with older members, we were advised to stop taking ourselves too seriously and to acquaint ourselves with the program before we started rewriting it.

They told us personalities were not changed overnight and we should be more open-minded and patient in working out the many details of our recovery.

Later, we learned the Twelve Steps progressively helped us to gain this end. As we lived them regularly, they tore down the mental barriers of prejudice and self-will that we had set up between God and ourselves. Eventually this living brought about a spiritual awakening that opened our eyes and gave us an entirely new outlook on life's true values.

We should work toward this revitalizing experience and arrange our lives around it. To miss this help only gives greater power to the problems that already have us down.

Alcoholics who serve themselves instead of God invite all forms of trouble. They fall easy prey to mental or physical drunkenness—usually to both.

Occasionally, members assume a sense of false security from sober periods, gained through group association, but without spiritual help.

We call this the "free ride." It looks like the real thing but fails to stand up against adversity, resentment, or the physical craving for alcohol.

Daily spiritual growth, prompted by a desperate need for help, is the most effective protection against these urges. God's help, plus group association, aids this necessary growth. They are the requisites of a successful AA life. They tend to make us content to live without alcohol.

This is an important point, for the difference between contented and unhappy sobriety is often— that first drink.

It takes no mastermind to determine the source of power we draw upon in arresting our alcoholism. Evidence of a spiritual change in our lives can be detected in almost every thought and act.

What—aside from a spiritual awakening—could ease our fear, resentment, and dishonesty? What else could curb our mental obsession and physical craving to drink?

There should be no difficulty in recognizing the essence of a spiritual experience in the contented sobriety we enjoy, in the responsibility we daily assume, in attitudes of forgiveness, in the amends we make, in willingness to admit our mistakes, in our unselfish interest in helping sick alcoholics and other persons who are less fortunate than ourselves.

The spiritual aspects of our lives become even more convincing when we discover that these things are done without thought of personal glory or hope of material gain.

But, the outcome of spiritual living is never without reward. God declares His dividends—not in human coinage but in the divine currency of serenity.

Excerpts from our "Southern Friend" in the Big Book mention this serenity. It says, "God produces harmony in those who receive His Spirit and follow Its dictates. ... Today when I become more harmonized within, I become more in tune with all of God's wonderful creation. ... There are periods of darkness, but the stars are shining, no matter how dark the night. There are disturbances, but I have learned that if I seek patience and open-mindedness, understanding comes. And with it direction by the spirit of God. The dawn comes and with it more understanding... and the joy of living that is not disturbed by circumstances or by people around me."*

The benefits of Twelve Step living enlarge as we share them with others. We are wise to share them, for

---

*These excerpts are taken from pages 240 and 241 in the original edition of the Big Book. They do not appear in the Second and Third Editions.

we cannot suppress the spiritual gifts of AA and maintain satisfying sobriety.

Each worthy thought put into practice brings us a step nearer to God. The Twelve Steps all lead in that direction. They are like stepping-stones that we slowly progress over to greater awareness of His presence. They are the means by which we make a conscious contact with Him. They stand as spiritual bulwarks between us and lives of desperation and drunkenness. By practicing the Steps we gain the priceless gem of contented sobriety. It is ours to hold as long as we willingly share it with other alcoholics who sincerely seek our help.

SECOND DIVISION

"...we tried to carry this message to alcoholics..."

Trying to carry the message of AA to alcoholics who seek our help seems like a mandate from a Higher Power to the members of our fellowship. It is the premise upon which AA was founded.

Rendering this service, we immunize ourselves against taking that first drink. We help restore faith in God and physical health to drinkers who have lost all hope of recovery from their alcoholic condition. This spiritual grant should not be ignored.

God has entrusted recovering alcoholics with a

special gift of healing alcoholics who still suffer. This gift was not given to educators, doctors, or clergy members; it was granted to us so we might justify our right to live sober, normal lives by helping other alcoholics recover from their illness.

When we assume this responsibility of carrying the message, we do not consider it presumptuous to suggest a general outline for sponsoring newcomers in AA.

The following suggestions are based upon advice found in Chapter Seven of *Alcoholics Anonymous* and upon the experience of successful AA members who have followed that advice.

From their experiences we have learned that a true concept of our Twelfth Step obligation must be very broad to cover its purpose.

For purpose of identification it is helpful to distinguish between the daily acts of carrying the message and the more complex duties of sponsorship which the Big Book refers to as "working with others." Sponsorship is discussed in the next section of this chapter.

We can readily see that the member who sponsors carries the message, but a member can carry the message without sponsoring another alcoholic. In fact, much more time is spent on such AA activities than on sponsorship.

This works in the best interest of our fellowship. It gives everyone something to do, including the newcomer who may feel too inexperienced to be of any help.

There are many ways of carrying the message besides sponsorship. Some of these activities appear in the following list.

1. The most convincing message we can carry to alcoholics is our own example of contented sobriety.
2. Making calls with older members who are sponsoring a new member.
3. The example of regular attendance at AA meetings. Visiting outside AA meetings when we are away from home.
4. Making hospital calls upon members.
5. Telephone calls to new members.
6. Friendly talks with persons after meetings, particularly with newcomers or those who are having trouble living the program.
7. By owning *Alcoholics Anonymous*. By encouraging other alcoholics to buy and study it for AA understanding.
8. By lending our books or by passing out our literature to interested persons.

9. Assuming the duties and obligations that will help our fellowship.

10. Talking with relatives or associates of drinking alcoholics. (By explaining to them alcoholism is a disease and how we arrest it in AA.)

11. By telling the AA story to clergy members, doctors, judges, educators, employers, or police officials if we know them well enough to further the AA cause, or to help out a fellow member.

12. By speaking before other groups or conducting meetings in our own group.

13. By making a reasonable pledge of our energy, time, and money to the fellowship.

14. By our obvious belief that we have received help from a Higher Power.

15. By making AA our way of life.

Sponsorship: Working with Other Alcoholics

Sponsorship represents the ultimate in AA giving. By this sharing act, persons on reprieve from insanity or alcoholic death share their recovery with others who want to escape the same penalty. This act is not entirely charitable since to withhold help is to lose our own reprieves.

Sponsorship, the dynamic factor of AA growth, fills three definite requirements:

1. It helps us maintain contented sobriety.
2. It helps others arrest their alcoholism.
3. It kills complacency and progressively replenishes the ranks of our fellowship.

The principle of working with others is sound, as it is founded upon the ageless axiom, "Give and you shall receive."

Twelfth Step work integrates our personalities and aids spiritual development. We cannot act the daily role of good counselors, hiding our acts in anonymity, without finally becoming better persons for it.

Likewise, we gain many spiritual blessings as we give unselfishly of our time and experience to suffering alcoholics. These rewards are intangible but of inestimable worth, as they bring us peace of mind, self-respect, and sobriety.

The Big Book places real emphasis upon our need for carrying the message by saying, "...this is an experience you must not miss."[*] Sponsorship fulfills our need for active service and helps us keep sober.

---

[*] Read page 89, Chapter Seven, of *Alcoholics Anonymous.*

Members who try to render this service are faced with the perplexing question, "How do we sponsor best?" AA has no specific answer. Each member must plan his or her own method. As a result, there is indecision and often conflicting views about proper procedure.

There are many procedures, both good and bad, between which we can discern the right course to pursue. Some sponsors are tolerant to a point of harmful indulgence. Some are evangelists. There are the "easy does it" types who are satisfied with merely getting their prospect to a meeting. Others are more exacting in their demands. They work only with *real alcoholics* and insist their candidates give them full cooperation by trying to understand and practice the Twelve Steps of AA.

This lack of set rules or unified plans for working with others would be most frustrating to a member who had never sponsored without a good source of "know-how" and practical experience to draw upon.

Fortunately, no member will be confused or ignorant about the mechanics of sponsorship, if he or she studies the Big Book. It has all the answers. They can be found in several chapters: "Working with Others," "The Doctor's Opinion," "A Vision for You," "There Is a Solution," "The Family Afterward," and the forty-three histories of recovered alcoholics under "Personal Stories."

It is not difficult to establish a successful sponsorship procedure if we follow the suggestions given in these chapters. Our acceptance need not be on faith alone. We may safely draw upon the experience of our founders who offer the AA fellowship as evidence that their plan works.

Borrowing freely from their advice and drawing heavily upon their experience, we present this sponsorship guide, hoping it will help those who work with alcoholics.

The Sponsor

An honest interpretation of Step Twelve permits no altering of its principles. The simple wording of the Step implies its intent. It outlines the qualifications of a sponsor. It identifies the people we will work with and suggests a way of life to keep us capable of future sponsorship.

The first requisites of sponsorship are sobriety and a personality change based on an active concept of God's will. We qualify for these by living the Twelve Steps. This is followed by knowledge of the AA program and the purpose of Step Twelve. This is accomplished by working with a special group of people, namely *alcoholics*.

Following this plan brings success with our prospects. Deviating from it, we invite failure and AA headaches. Some say we go on trial each time we sponsor. The life of the newcomer and the future of AA could easily depend upon the quality of our sobriety and the manner in which we share it with other alcoholics.

Working with others is always a serious matter for AA and the prospect. First, they look to us for counsel to help them overcome their drinking problems; they then look to the AA program for rehabilitation of their lives.

Younger members can prepare themselves for sponsoring by a close study of Chapter Seven and other related chapters in the Big Book. Short on know-how, they will have to offset their lack of experience with knowledge and enthusiasm gained from older members. This brings up an important phase of carrying the message that we will comment upon briefly.

Double Sponsorship

The value of double sponsorship has been recognized by many groups. Some now make it their standard practice. Examples of its effectiveness started with AA's inception.

Bill W. had little success with alcoholics until he and Dr. Bob started working with them together. The need for dual sponsorship is just as great today.

Among its advantages are such things as preparedness, safety in numbers, efficiency, good presentation, and better follow-up.

From the standpoint of preparedness, two members can plan and follow a better course of action than one. Paired up, we lessen the element of danger and provide work for a younger member. The prospect gets two views of AA. Follow-up is more complete.

An older member with a successful record of working with alcoholics never sponsors alone. He always calls in a younger person to help him and insists they both read Chapter Seven before making the call, except in emergency cases. The results have been helpful for the prospect and for the younger member who, in turn, makes this practice his or her own future sponsorship procedure.

Literally defined, a sponsor is one who willingly binds him- or herself to answer for another's default. The AA interpretation differs in that we bind ourselves to help the newcomer answer for his or her own default by indoctrination to a new way of life.

Those of us who sponsor improve our pattern of procedure with each new experience. There are many things to learn about helping the alcoholic "who still suffers." Foremost among these is knowing the quality of our own sobriety.

We should be critical of our own development in this respect, as it is impossible to share qualities that we do not possess ourselves.

On the other hand, even though we are well qualified, we cannot share AA with alcoholics who reject our help. It is pointless to try. We drop them for a while but leave the AA door open, so they may call later if they have a change of heart.

Considering this aspect of sponsorship, it seems prospective members must have definite qualifications to be eligible for our fellowship. Such is the case, but the qualifications are extremely limited. The alcoholic's "only requirement for membership is an honest desire to stop drinking."* There are other minor qualifications for membership in special groups, but the main requirement is the same for all.

Another significant part of sponsorship, in which several members can carry the message, is that of starting new groups or working with weaker ones. We need this service which, in turn, strengthens us by

---

*See page xiv in the "Foreword to the First Edition" in *Alcoholics Anonymous*.

giving our members a constructive outlet for their latent AA energies.

Although the benefits from working with others are shared mutually by the sponsor and the prospect (whether it be an individual or a group), we seldom think about ourselves when making a Twelfth Step call.

Herein lies a cardinal virtue of sponsorship. It is the momentary loss of self-centeredness. This attitude, engendered by a desire to share our recovery with other alcoholics, is a sign of healthy AA growth. As we share, we grow in AA stature and increase our chances for a happy, sober life.

Every AA member is a potential sponsor, and most members aspire to sponsor successfully. Our great ambition is to help alcoholics recover from their illness. Success often rewards our efforts, but we never get discouraged if the prospect fails to cooperate. Many calls must be made before we find an alcoholic desperate enough to accept AA. Our duty is to find them. How is this done? Where can they be located?

Locating Prospective Members

A successful harmonious plan for locating AA prospects and for constructive future work with them can be easily established by any progressive AA group.

An explicit outline for such a plan is given in Chapter Seven of the Big Book. Wise members will agree to adopt it as an authoritative guide for sponsorship. Thus they work in unison, with all members having the same source of our founders' experience at their command.

There are many sources to reach prospective members. Widespread AA publicity provides contacts through telephone and written requests. This important service has greatly enlarged our fellowship. Its value is well established, but members regress who depend upon it alone.

All members must carry the message to develop AA's growth and gain personal experience if we are to continue the source of referrals started by our founders.

How is this accomplished? Find your answer in the Big Book. Read paragraph three in the chapter, "Working with Others." It says, "Perhaps you are not acquainted with any drinkers who want to recover. You can easily find some by asking a few doctors, ministers, priests, or hospitals. They will be only too glad to assis. you."

Good public relations reward such efforts and eventually start requests for help by alcoholics who need AA. We gain the most from following these calls because we have had a part in their making.

By educating doctors, the clergy, judges, police officials, and industrial personnel regarding the type of people AA can help, we will avoid flooding our ranks with an unwieldy preponderance of nonalcoholics.

Inquiries from the families of alcoholics are often overlooked as a means of locating new prospects. If an alcoholic wants no part of AA, we can still carry the message to inquiring relatives.

Those who ask for help are entitled to an explanation of the disease, alcoholism. We should tell them about the Twelve Steps and how the program will work for the sick member of their family if that person will accept it.

They will find a means of enlightening alcoholics. Leave them some AA literature, and you will have planted a seed in their minds that may develop a good future prospect for AA.

Other sources of prospective members for AA can be developed through newspapers, radio, and television.

Tact and good judgment must be used, however, as no publicity is far better than bad publicity that might harm AA or rob it of dignity and appeal. In all public relation contacts our principle of anonymity should be thoroughly understood. It is our obligation to see that it is respected.

All groups should consider their objectives and motives before releasing a publicity program.

We must protect our personal anonymity. Motives prompted by a desire to exalt AA or its members are wrong. Our aim is service. By the principle of attraction, we can help those who suffer from alcoholism find their way into AA.

Helpful Hints for Sponsors

The following suggestions are from data found in Chapter Seven of the Big Book. We trust they will prove helpful as a supplementary guide for study of that chapter.

Certainly, the most impressive thing we have to offer the prospect is our example of a sober, happy, and purposeful life.

Remember the prospect is sick in body, mind, and spirit; we, alone, can help this person recover.

Alcoholics minimize their drinking when interviewed before relatives, so see them privately if you can. The family can fill in additional facts later. To help the alcoholic, we must know his or her type of drinking, habits, hobbies, religion, business, financial condition, and what cooperation to expect from the family.

If the alcoholic needs hospital care, help the person get it by making the necessary arrangements.

We should tell our stories and get newcomers to tell theirs. Avoiding evangelism, we explain how AA functions, how it worked for us. and how it can work for them. Stress anonymity. Label alcoholism as an illness.

Leave AA literature if a prospect is interested. Suggest he or she call after reading it. If the person believes he or she is alcoholic and wants to join our fellowship, suggest reading the Big Book. We should not push the person into AA. Let the alcoholic ask for it.

The newcomer should know about the spiritual aspect of AA, particularly that it is not a religion but one's own concept of God as we understand Him.

When the newcomer indicates willingness to join AA just to help the family, discourage the idea. Explain why it won't work. Point out alcoholism is an illness that the person must recover from; he or she is sick, not the family.

The alcoholic's family should not be ignored. Tell them why the AA program will become a part of the prospect's daily life. Invite their cooperation. It often makes the difference between success and failure.

Problems involving the lending of money, keeping alcoholics in our homes, divorce, spiritual development, family quarrels, and shunning drinking places are explained on pages 96-103, Chapter Seven of the Big Book. It is well to study them in preparation for these contingencies.

Recognize the sick and lonely condition of the alcoholic. Be friendly, but don't coddle the person. Treat each case with reason. Although we may help the newcomer to a meeting at first, we choose not to make it a fixed habit. Emphasize the need to attend meetings. Portray the opportunity as a lifesaving privilege, and nothing must deter us.

Be worthy of the prospect's trust. Counsel the person wisely; advise the purchase of a Big Book. See that the prospect studies it for a better understanding of this new way of life.

Teach the newcomer the value of Twelve Step living and reliance on God's help for recovery. Newcomers should not lean upon us too heavily or they may fail to develop enough AA strength to succeed with our program.

Advice to the Newcomer

For the best results, consider yourself a patient in AA for the arrest of an incurable disease. Determine to get the utmost from your treatment. Go on the theory that AA can do without you, but that you cannot live without AA. Avoid unreasonable demands upon your sponsor. Never get the idea that by slipping you let your sponsor down. You are the person who will suffer. God is the one you will let down.

Buy a Big Book and follow its advice. It is foolish to assume you can recover from alcoholism without a book which contains the recovery instructions.

Abstain from weakening the AA program with Twelve Step substitutions, or you will water it down to a point of drunkenness.

Don't take AA lightly. It may be your last chance for sanity or sobriety. Your decision to live the AA program is important. Put nothing ahead of it. Approach it with honesty, humility, open-mindedness, willingness, and appreciation.

THIRD DIVISION

"...and to practice these principles in all our affairs."

The principles of the Twelve Steps add up to a logical and livable way of life which will restore health, happiness, and sobriety to sick hopeless alcoholics.

Hundreds of thousands of members who have recovered from alcoholism give living proof that the AA program works for those who apply it.

We work for daily recovery which is all that we expect. Experience has taught us we cannot drink normally again.

Our heritage of sane living is denied until we fully recognize and start treating our alcoholism as a physical, mental, and spiritual illness.

Our heritage is restored when we:

1. Acknowledge our physical and mental illness and work for recovery.
2. Seek help from God as we understand Him to arrest our spiritual illness.
3. Study and isolate our defects of character with a view to correcting them.
4. Admit these defects to ourselves and to God and talk them over with another person.
5. Rely upon the Twelve Steps to inspire us with worthy motives.
6. Concede the injury that our drinking addiction has inflicted upon others.
7. Ask God's forgiveness for these acts and make amends to the persons harmed.
8. Develop the habit of admitting our mistakes and correcting our character defects.
9 Cultivate better spiritual relations with God and try to execute His will.

10. Share the experience of our recovery with alcoholics who ask for help.
11. Continue living the AA life by practicing "these principles in all our affairs."

For the convenience of members interested in further consideration of carrying the message to alcoholics, this suggested list of questions and answers from the Third Edition of *Alcoholics Anonymous* may provide helpful information.

Carrying the message to alcoholics has general acceptance as good AA procedure. How was the "message" carried to Bill W., the founder of our fellowship? (Answer) Bill's Story, last two paragraphs of page 8.

How important is sponsorship to recovery? Should we consider it a "must"? (Answers) Page 89, paragraph two; page 14, last paragraph, through page 15, first paragraph; page 97, first paragraph; page 102, lines 7-8.

AA has helped reclaim the lives of countless alcoholics. Does this imply that every alcoholic who asks for help can recover? (Answer) Page 163, last paragraph.

From what source will our future membership come? How are we to find them? (Answers) Page 89, paragraph three; page 155, lines 1-6; page 162, lines 8-11; pages 163, 185, 302.

How essential are our examples of contented sobriety to the alcoholic seeking AA help? (Answers) Page 18, last two paragraphs; page 89, first paragraph; page 180, lines 17-23; page 235, paragraphs one and two.

Some AA prospects toy with the idea of controlled drinking. Some are undecided if they are alcoholic. Does the Big Book offer a test for determining their conditions? (Answer) Page 31, last paragraph, through page 32.

When—if ever—do we drop a prospective member? (Answers) Page 95, paragraph two; page 96, first paragraph.

What is the requirement for membership in AA? (Answer) Page xiv, "Foreword to First Edition."

Is our program for those other than alcoholics? (Answers) Page xiii, first paragraph, "Foreword to First Edition"; page 17, last paragraph; page 25, last paragraph; page 29, last paragraph; page 30, paragraph two; page 38, last paragraph; page 39, first paragraph; page 60, first paragraph; page 92; page 96, first paragraph.

Do our stories have inducement value to prospective AA members? (Answers) Page 17, last paragraph; page 157, lines 15-29; page 180, second paragraph; page 495, first paragraph.

What is the first step of an alcoholic's recovery? (Answer) Page 30, second paragraph.

Is hospitalization important to an alcoholic's recovery? (Answers) See page xxiv, "The Doctor's Opinion," last paragraph; page 91, first and second paragraphs; page 133, second paragraph.

When we find a prospect for AA what is the exact procedure to approach the prospect? (Answer) Read pages 90-103.

If we need information about a prospect's health, finance, religion, drinking habits—where do we get it? (Answer) Page 90, first and second paragraphs.

Do we always try to stop a prospect from drinking—or is it sometimes best that the person goes on another binge? (Answer) Page 90, third paragraph.

Do we deal with alcoholics when they are very drunk or ugly? (Answer) Page 90, third paragraph.

Do we ever force ourselves upon an alcoholic and insist that he or she stop drinking? (Answer) Page 90, last paragraph.

Do we call upon the new person who is still jittery and

depressed? (Answer) Page 91, second paragraph.

Do we see the new person alone, or in the presence of his or her family? (Answer) Page 91, first and second paragraphs.

When do we refer to alcoholism as a sickness—a fatal malady? (Answer) Page 91, last paragraph and first paragraph on page 92.

If your prospect is an agnostic or atheist how do you begin to discuss God? (Answer) Page 93, lines 4-10.

Is AA a religion? How do we explain this to a newcomer? (Answer) Page 93, last line, through first paragraph on page 94.

Assume that you are working with a prospective member. When do you lend that person a copy of the book, Alcoholics Anonymous? (Answer) Page 94, last paragraph.

Assume that the prospect seems overanxious to join AA. What action do we take? (Answer) Page 95, first paragraph.

Does AA recommend that we act as nurse and banker for the newcomer? (Answer) Page 97, last line; and page 98.

Is the newcomer advised to read Alcoholics Anonymous *before coming into AA?* (Answer) Page 95, third paragraph.

When discouraged with alcoholics who will not respond to help, what do we do? (Answer) Page 95, last paragraph, through first paragraph on page 96.

How discreetly do we handle the prospect who is homeless and broke? (Answer) Page 96, last paragraph.

When, if ever, do we let alcoholics live in our homes? (Answer) Page 97, first and second paragraphs.

Separation is often encountered. What if a newcomer says he or she cannot recover without the family? (Answer) Page 99, last paragraph.

Should the sponsor help in family rows? (Answer) Page 100, second and third paragraphs.

How do members meet circumstances requiring their presence where liquor is served? (Answer) Page 100, last paragraph; pages 101-102.

What is organized religion's attitude toward AA? (Answer) Page 574.

What is medicine's view on AA? (Answer) Pages 571-572.

We often refer to spiritual awakenings and spiritual experiences in AA. What do we mean by this? (Answer) Pages 569-570.

STOOLS AND BOTTLES

Stools and Bottles is a 160-page illustrated book of sound AA principles. It exposes many barriers to our recovery from alcoholism and suggests ways of overcoming them.

Stools and Bottles has been well received by AA members worldwide. It is most helpful for outlining a written inventory before taking Step Five. You may want to encourage the person who is hearing your Fifth Step to read it beforehand.

Appendix: B
We Don't Have To—But!

In desperation, we joined AA for one purpose: to get sober. Sobriety was not forced on us. Our Twelve Step recovery program was entirely suggestive.

By humble daily practice of this program we achieved sobriety. Then God performed an added miracle. God threw in peace of mind for good measure, plus security and happiness for our families.

Living the Twelve Steps was not compulsory, yet as we grew in understanding of our new way of life, we realized it embraced many voluntary "musts."

It is interesting to check some of these "musts" which are found in *Alcoholics Anonymous*. We offer them as noteworthy requisites for successful AA living.

Listed below are a few of them to be found in the Third Edition of *Alcoholics Anonymous*.

1. Physical illness. Page xxiv, second paragraph.
2. Self-centeredness. Page 62, line 18.
3. Self-destruction. Page 62, line 19.
4. Resentment. Page 66, line 30.
5. Sex. Page 69, paragraph four.
6. Step Five. Page 74, line 4.
7. Procrastination. Page 75, line 1.
8. Fear of creditors. Page 78, line 23.
9. Amends. Page 79, paragraph one.
10. Omissions. Page 80, paragraph two.
11. Is sobriety enough? Page 82, line 17.
12. Family reconstruction. Page 83, first paragraph.

Daily recovery from alcoholism is possible providing we are desperate enough to go to any lengths to get well.

We "can only be defeated by an attitude of intolerance or belligerent denial.... *Willingness, honesty and openmindedness are the essentials of recovery. But these are indispensable.*"[*]

---

[*]Taken from the closing remarks, "Spiritual Experience," on page 570 of *Alcoholics Anonymous*.

About Hazelden Publishing

As part of the Hazelden Betty Ford Foundation, Hazelden Publishing offers both cutting-edge educational resources and inspirational books. Our print and digital works help guide individuals in treatment and recovery, and their loved ones. Professionals who work to prevent and treat addiction also turn to Hazelden Publishing for evidence-based curricula, digital content solutions, and videos for use in schools, treatment programs, correctional programs, and electronic health records systems. We also offer training for implementation of our curricula.

Through published and digital works, Hazelden Publishing extends the reach of healing and hope to individuals, families, and communities affected by addiction and related issues.

For more information about Hazelden publications,
please call **800-328-9000**
or visit us online at **hazelden.org/bookstore.**

Other titles that will interest you…

Twenty-Four Hours a Day

Nothing talks like the truth. And nothing tells it better than this classic meditation book. The practice of daily meditation in recovery began with this inspiring resource—still as powerful today as it was over 60 years ago. Each day of the year, *Twenty-Four Hours a Day* provides an A.A. Thought for the Day, a short meditation on living the Twelve Step program, and a prayer. Paperback, 400 pp.
Order No. 5093

Stools and Bottles

From the author of *The Little Red Book* comes a memorable early A.A. lecture about the first three Steps. The power of the Steps and the problems caused by character defects are clearly illustrated using a three-legged stool and eight whiskey bottles. Also included are 31 daily meditations to help us focus on common stumbling blocks in early recovery. Hardcover, 160 pp.
Order No. 1040

A Program for You
A Guide to the Big Book's Design for Living

Written in today's language, this study guide interprets the original A.A. program and helps us apply it to our lives. *A Program for You* brings the entire Big Book to life through discussion and page references, revealing that the Twelve Steps remain a key to successful living. 183 pp.
Order No. 5122

For more information about Hazelden publications,
Please call **800-328-9000**
Or visit us online at **hazelden.org/bookstore.**